SAVING JUSTICE

SAVING JUSTICE

Watergate, the Saturday Night Massacre, and Other Adventures of a Solicitor General

---

ROBERT H. BORK

Encounter Books
New York • London

First American edition published in 2013 by Encounter Books, an activity of Encounter for Culture and Education, Inc., a nonprofit, tax-exempt corporation.
Encounter Books website address: www.encounterbooks.com

Manufactured in the United States and printed on acid-free paper. The paper used in this publication meets the minimum requirements of ANSI/NISO Z39.48–1992 (R 1997) (*Permanence of Paper*).

FIRST AMERICAN EDITION

Produced by Wilsted & Taylor Publishing Services

LIBRARY OF CONGRESS CATALOGING-IN-PUBLICATION DATA
Bork, Robert H.
Saving Justice : Watergate, the Saturday night massacre, and other adventures of a Solicitor General / Robert Bork.
pages cm
Includes bibliographical references and index.
ISBN-13: 978-1-59403-681-1 (hardcover : alk. paper)
ISBN-10: 1-59403-681-0 (hardcover : alk. paper)
ISBN-13: 978-1-59403-518-0 (ebook)
1. Bork, Robert H. 2. United States. Solicitor General. 3. United States. Dept. of Justice—Officials and employees—Biography. 4. Watergate Affair, 1972–1974. I. Title.
KF373.B57A3 2013
973.924092—dc23
[B]
2012047634

To Bea Kristol

CONTENTS

FOREWORD

It is not an exaggeration to describe Robert H. Bork as one of our nation's greatest legal minds. Upon his recent death, publications throughout the country paid tribute to him as a "champion of the Constitution" and an "iconic conservative judge." One national newspaper called him a "pivotal figure in Supreme Court history." It went on to state that Judge Bork was not only a legal theorist but also a "highly regarded constitutional lawyer" whom Supreme Court justices have praised as "one of the finest advocates they had ever seen."

It is this rich background of professional accomplishment that Robert Bork brings to the writing of *Saving Justice: Watergate, the Saturday Night Massacre, and Other Adventures of a Solicitor General.* But to really appreciate the historic events depicted here, it is important to understand the character and background of the author, since this narrative is more than an account of leadership during a legal and political crisis. This is also a chronicle of ethical conduct, dedicated public service, and devotion to the rule of law.

Even the *New York Times* described Robert Bork as "a multifaceted man with a powerful and restless intellect." Perhaps the most comprehensive appraisal of his accomplishments appeared in the *National Review Online*:

> Had Robert H. Bork never been nominated to the nation's highest court, he would still have been an important figure in American law. As a professor at Yale Law School; as a scholar who blazed a trail of reform of antitrust jurisprudence and made important contributions to the emergence of originalism in constitutional law; as a highly regarded solicitor general who stepped in to be acting attorney general at a moment of political crisis; and as an appellate judge who improved the D.C. Circuit Court of Appeals by his presence on it, Bork made his mark on the theory and practice of American law before Ronald Reagan ever sent the Senate his nomination to be an associate justice of the Supreme Court.

Robert Bork's service to the United States began even before he became a lawyer. As a seventeen-year-old, he enlisted in the Marine Corps during World War II and after college served again, as a Marine officer. This experience provided him with a valuable understanding of the variety of people and the broader society in our country.

In the private practice of law and then as law professor at

the Yale School of Law, Bork's work in antitrust law became so widely recognized that it changed the way this whole field of jurisprudence was regarded by academicians and the legal profession itself. During this time, he began shaping his views on constitutional and statutary interpretation. His scholarship produced the conclusion that for our republic to be "a government of laws, rather than of men," judges must base their decisions on the firm foundation of the Constitution and statutes enacted by the people's representatives.

This reasoning led to a 1971 article in the *Indiana Law Journal* on the responsibility of judges to interpret the Constitution, and statutes enacted pursuant to it, according to the original understanding of those who drafted, enacted, or ratified them. Judge Bork quickly became one of the foremost champions of this doctrine of "constitutional fidelity" or "originalism" as it has developed over the past several decades. He criticized judges or justices who engaged in "judicial activism" by substituting their personal biases, political views, or policy preferences for judicial decisions that reflected what the Constitution or laws actually provided.

It was this championing of the Founders' doctrine of "judicial restraint" that, later in Bork's career, was a major factor in President Ronald Reagan's decision to nominate him to serve on the United States Court of Appeals for the District of Columbia Circuit, and subsequently to select Bork for elevation to the U.S. Supreme Court in 1987.

As a lawyer, law professor, and judge, Robert Bork gained a reputation among his professional colleagues, students, and law clerks as a sound thinker, a person of strong ethical character, and a friendly confidant and advisor. He was firm in his convictions but was respected by, and able to work well with, others who did not share his views on law or political philosophy. His interest in guiding and assisting young lawyers was demonstrated by his active participation in and mentoring of the Federalist Society, an organization established in 1982 to promote policy discussion and debate in law schools and among its lawyer chapters. For several years Bork served as co-chairman of its advisory board.

The previous exposition of Bork's philosophy and career explains and verifies his principled conduct that forms the narrative of *Saving Justice.* Unexpectedly called to duty in the Department of Justice as solicitor general, he gave up a comfortable position as a law professor to take on a risky and demanding job at a time of great turmoil in our nation. Out of a sense of duty, he was willing to accept a responsibility that in today's vernacular we would say was definitely not a "career-enhancing" move.

In 1973 the nation's capital was immersed in what became known as "the Watergate affairs." During the previous year's presidential election campaign, the burglary of Democratic Party headquarters, and accusations of a subsequent cover-up involving several White House officials—possibly even the president—became a major political and legal issue.

Responding to massive demand in Congress and from the news media for an independent inquiry into the Watergate allegations, President Nixon directed the appointment of a special prosecutor to investigate the various charges. This official was to serve under the authority of the attorney general but was to operate separately and independently from the rest of the Department of Justice.

This was the situation when President Nixon appointed Robert Bork to fill a vacancy in the Justice Department as solicitor general, that agency's third-ranking official and the lawyer responsible for overseeing all of the nation's appellate litigation. Ordinarily the person holding this position would not have been involved in matters related to the Watergate investigation. But when the Watergate inquiry produced a major dispute between the president and the special prosecutor, Bork was suddenly thrust into the leadership of the Department of Justice and confronted with numerous challenges of law and executive responsibility. This story forms the basis for *Saving Justice,* which provides a fascinating and inspiring account of principled leadership and professional conduct, which served our nation well in a time of crisis.

But Robert Bork's contributions to the cause of justice did not end there. After his work as solicitor general, he returned to teaching law school until 1982, when he was appointed by Ronald Reagan to a judgeship on the District of Columbia appellate court. There he transformed his constitutional jurisprudence into judicial practice, which resulted in President Reagan nominating him for the Supreme Court in 1987.

When Ronald Reagan selected Robert Bork to replace Lewis Powell, who had retired as an associate justice, the nomination was described as a move that "set the Senate afire" and led to "a historic political battle whose impact is still being felt" decades later. Despite the fact that Judge

Bork was one of the most qualified persons ever nominated for the Supreme Court and despite his impeccable character and distinguished credentials, a coalition of extreme leftist organizations turned what had historically been a civil and dignified confirmation process into a vicious political battle. The majority of the Senate had just changed from Republican to Democrat, and these ultra-liberal groups had organized for a bitter fight. In less than an hour after the announcement of Bork's nomination, a prominent senator who was a virulent opponent of the Reagan administration on almost every issue took to the floor of the Senate and delivered a torrent of falsehoods. This speech was followed by a deluge of false propaganda and an anti-Bork effort that even included negative television commercials in the states of key senators.

As a result, to the shame of the Senate, the Bork nomination was defeated. The *New York Times* described the unprecedented campaign as a "watershed event" that "is widely seen to have shifted the tone and emphasis of Supreme Court nominations since then, giving them an often strong political cast and making it hard, many argue, for a nominee with firmly held views ever to be confirmed." Another observer commented that "the Senate's abysmal performance denied the nation a justice of towering intellect and abiding fidelity to the idea that is, or was, America."

Obviously, this unfair and undeserved setback was a disappointment to Judge Bork, his family, and his many supporters. A lesser person might have given up on the nation and on public service. But Robert Bork—who showed his strength of character in this ordeal as he did throughout his career—returned to serving his country and to defending the rule of law. As columnist Andrew McCarthy has written, Judge Bork became "an unparalleled legal, moral, and ethical philosopher in a time dominated by a law-culture corrosive to moral and ethical moorings."

In recent years this man has provided the nation a rich legacy of best-selling books, articles, teaching, and speeches that involve a critique of the culture, insightful commentary on the law, and advocacy in support of the Founders' Constitution. An important part of this legacy is *Saving Justice,* in which Robert Bork has performed a great public service by providing an accurate and understandable account of how the integrity and responsibility of the Department of Justice was upheld, how constitutional government was protected, and how the rule of law was preserved. For that, and for his principled leadership in making it happen, we should all be grateful.

EDWIN MEESE III
January 2013

Edwin Meese III served as the seventy-fifth attorney general of the United States from 1985 to 1988. He is currently the Ronald Reagan Distinguished Fellow Emeritus at the Heritage Foundation in Washington, D.C.

ACKNOWLEDGMENTS

My husband, Robert, died on December 19, 2012, before he could write his acknowledgments. This is a list of people who were colleagues in the Solicitor General's office, friends, or those who assisted him in other ways that he wanted to acknowledge.

Mary Ellen Bork
January 3, 2013

Sara Sun Beale, Danny J. Boggs, Frank Easterbrook, H. Bartow Farr, Andrew Frey, Daniel M. Friedman, Paul L. Friedman, Kenneth S. Geller, Keith A. Jones, Edmund Kitch, Edward R. Korman, Jewel Lafontant, Jerry Norton, A. Raymond Randolph, Robert Reich, Harry Sachse, Harriet Shapiro, Howard E. Shapiro, Stuart A. Smith, Allan Tuttle, Steve Urbanczyk, Lawrence G. Wallace, and Judy Carper

Judge Ralph K. Winter, Jr., Alex Bickel

The Nixon Library

The Library of Congress, Law Library

Research assistants: Darren Beattie, Mitchell Boersma, Arthur Ewenczyk, Matthew Glover, Harley Metcalfe III, and Adam Steene

Courtesy of the author

Robert H. Bork with President Richard Nixon
at Camp David on December 12, 1972.

PROLOGUE

The Office of Solicitor General

WHEN I CAME TO WASHINGTON to assume the office of solicitor general in the last days of June 1973, I had no intimation of the events into which I would soon be plunged. As the columnist William L. Safire put it, I had to hit the ground running. Within weeks of my arrival, even before I had time to settle into my office, I had to deal with President Richard Nixon's request that I resign as solicitor general and become his chief defense attorney, respond to Supreme Court Justice William O. Douglas's order that our military stop bombing in Cambodia, file briefings for the prosecution of Vice President Spiro T. Agnew for taking bribes while governor of Maryland, discharge Archibald Cox as special prosecutor in the Watergate affair, and secure the continuity of the Watergate investigation until we found a replacement for Cox. Thankfully, I was spared from dealing with the Yom Kippur War in the Middle East, which occupied others in the administration at the time. Needless to say, there was a sense of urgency pervading the administration.

This book is not a history of the Nixon administration, nor a biography of the man. It is a recounting of episodes that occurred while I was involved as a member of the Nixon administration during the last half of 1973 and the first few months of 1974. My object is not a formal statement, but rather a narrative of the events I was concerned with leading up to and as a member of the administration.

Few people outside the Washington bar fully understand the office of solicitor general. Some confuse the tasks of the solicitor general with those of the attorney general.

The attorney general administers a vast complex of enforcement agencies that are part of the Department of Justice, such as the Criminal Division, the Civil Division, the Antitrust Division, and the Tax Division (among others), as well as more than ninety United States attorneys and their offices around the nation, the Federal Bureau of Investigation (FBI), and the Immigration and Naturalization Service (INS). The Justice Department is a huge bureaucracy, with funding of $28.2 billion in 2012.

The solicitor general is the chief appellate advocate for the United States government. His primary responsibility is to represent the federal government before the Supreme Court. The Department's lawyers represent executive branch agencies of government in their litigation throughout the federal and state courts, and occasionally some of the independent regulatory agencies, such as the Securities and Exchange Commission (SEC) and the National Labor Relations Board (NLRB), before the Supreme Court. Besides arguing cases before the Supreme Court, the solicitor general also plays a crucial role in directing the federal government's litigation. With the power to say whether cases that the government has lost in the lower courts should go forward or be dropped, the solicitor general exercises substantial control over the flow of cases, as well as the issues that will be presented to the appellate courts.

The solicitor general deals with a wealth of cases, ranging from the most complex and weighty matters (during my term we dealt with the constitutionality of the death penalty) down to the legality of a simple tax lien laid on a government entity by a state. Of course, the growth of the administrative state plunges the solicitor general into all kinds of cases in which he has no real expertise or interest. For example, the central issue in one of the cases I argued concerned the seabed between the Atlantic coast and the drop-off of the continental shelf. Suffice it to say I was not intimately familiar with the topic.

I had only been solicitor general six weeks when I told a group of antitrust lawyers that it was the best job I'd ever had. The position embodies the ideal combination of intellectuality and action that draws people to the law in the first place. At the heart of the law lies the conflict between the ideal of liberty and the ideal of equality, which I think is inescapable in any human society. Those are themes that cross every lawyer's desk, but they cross the solicitor general's desk every day in cases of stunning and bewildering complexity and variety. They are presented as they should be in Anglo-Saxon jurisprudence, not as abstractions but as ultimate issues embedded in very particularized factual settings and very specific controversies. That is why I think the job combines the best of practice and the best of the academic world.

A bit about the day-to-day operation while I occupied the position from 1973 to 1977: It was a very small office. There were fourteen lawyers on the staff, including four deputies. Each of these deputies was assigned to a particular subject matter, a particular Division of the Department. The assistants, the other ten lawyers, were not specialized and were called to work upon any type of case, as may the solicitor general, who is also nonspecialized. At first I was astounded by the number of subjects that went flying across my desk in which I was meant to be an expert, such as the Atlantic continental shelf case I mentioned earlier, or briefs on Indian treaties. But I got used to that quickly.

Then as today, cases came to us from the various Divisions of the Department and from almost all of the agencies, and they came in various ways. The solicitor general's office had to approve all appeals, from district courts and courts of appeals, in cases the government had lost at trial level. It involved reviewing the entire file and making a decision about whether it called for an appeal. The solicitor general's office also had to approve, after a government loss in a court of appeals, all petitions for rehearing, suggestions for rehearing *en banc* (a rehearing before all judges of a court instead of just a panel), and, of course, all government appeals and petitions for *certiorari* to the Supreme Court. Beyond that, we would then write the petitions, the jurisdictional statements, the opposition to *certiorari* where the government had won below, plus all briefs on the merits.

To give you some idea of the flow during 1973, this rather small office made about 2,000 decisions concerning whether or not the government should appeal. Many of these decisions were extremely difficult and required the resolution of conflicting philosophies of different agencies and divisions. I averaged one such conference a week and escaped relatively unscathed, but it was impossible to arrive at an amicable settlement every time. In addition to these few thousand appellate decisions, we filed pleadings or briefs in about 1,700 cases in 1973. Of these, we fully briefed and argued a little more than half of the cases on the merits. These 900 cases made up about two-thirds of the entire caseload in the Supreme Court. We were, and still are, far and away the largest litigant in the Court. Needless to say, the solicitor general does not argue all of those cases. The office assigns arguments to particular persons, all of whom are good lawyers.

Oral argument in front of the Supreme Court ranks low as a spectator sport, though it can be engrossing for the direct participants, judges and lawyers who are intimately familiar with the state of play. The third-party observer rarely knows the intricacies of the case: the legal terrain over which it is fought, the danger points for the advocates, the skill (or lack thereof) with which the lawyer finesses the difficulties and attempts to turn the case his way. And after all that, the Court reserves judgment and leaves the room without announcing a decision until months later. For that reason, the memorable oral arguments are usually the disastrous ones.

The main problem in the office is a staggering workload that has become steadily and rapidly worse through the years. It has to be experienced to be believed. Six weeks into the job, I told that same group of antitrust lawyers they were under the misapprehension that I was wearing a beard. "I am not wearing a beard," I told them. "There just hasn't been time to shave, and this is a six-week stubble."

This problem of workload was not confined to my office. The accelerating flood of federal litigation ran all of the litigating divisions ragged, and does so to this day. The federal courts at all levels experience similar difficulties.

While the litigating divisions can ease their troubles when the budget increases by adding more lawyers, the solicitor general's office faces a special problem. Although the flow of appeals and petitions to the Supreme Court continually increases, the number of cases accepted for full briefing and argument does not. The office attracts highly gifted young lawyers to handle this massive workload with the promise of a few Supreme Court arguments every year. Therefore, the solicitor general cannot increase the staff materially, because that would dilute the number of arguments that could go to any one lawyer, which would make the office much less attractive.

An enormous number of cases could be cut out but, as I discovered, an equally large amount of cases cannot. For example, there are a great many diversity jurisdiction cases—where jurisdiction is exercised because the parties are in different states with conflicting laws on the same matter. I tried to get rid of those cases on the grounds that enmity between the states had been on the decline ever since the Constitution was written, and had reached a point where diversity jurisdiction was not really necessary to protect litigants against prejudice. But I was proved wrong. As one lawyer from Colorado told me: "If you insist on arguing [the local case], you're gonna have to eat the home cookin'."

The sheer flow of the work has another undesirable effect. It is increasingly more difficult for the solicitor general to find the time to involve himself very deeply in any particular case. The cases seem to come in at a rapid-fire rate, and all you have time to do is read the brief and send it out the door. For that reason the solicitor general often lacks the time to shape cases and through his litigation strategy to assist the Court in shaping legal doctrine; yet I think that is probably the most crucial function the office can serve, and is the function in which I was most interested.

On the whole, I was able to rearrange the flow of cases in the office in such a way that I was not relegated to the status of a proofreader. There was a point when I feared I might have to abandon the long-standing tradition of the solicitor general reading every word of every pleading that goes to the Supreme Court—about six pleadings a day, every day, including Saturdays and Sundays. Ultimately, I was able to fit it all in. In fact, more often than not I managed to find time to do the crossword puzzle in the mornings—a ritual that amused the staff. But I don't recall cutting any reading I needed to do. Maybe I just got faster as time went on. While I continued to read every case, I found that I handled matters more quickly as time passed.

Another difficulty of the office is getting hold of important cases early enough. The Department of Justice is organized in horizontal layers, so that one attorney handles the trial, a second the presentation to the court of appeals, and a third the presentation to the Supreme Court. I am convinced that structure is necessary. It is not like a private law office. It can't have a group or team of lawyers who handle a case all the way from the trial level to the Supreme Court, for one reason: somebody has to coordinate the policies in these cases and make sure they are consistent, and at the Supreme Court level that is the solicitor general's office. We cannot have the government taking conflicting positions. The process has to be coordinated, and that implies horizontal layering.

The solicitor general's office is also under an obligation, I think, to protect the Supreme Court against the filing of relatively trivial and frivolous appeals and petitions for *certiorari*, because the Court's workload is heavy enough. But as a result of this horizontal layering of the Department, the office is quite frequently completely unaware when a crucial constitutional issue is presented to a trial court. The case may be successfully defended on the pleadings or with a few affidavits, and then the office suddenly finds itself in the Supreme Court on the other side of a petition, litigating abstract issues on the basis of our opponent's allegation of facts. In order to prevent inadequate records leading to oversimplistic and sweeping constitutional doctrine, I tried to insert some forms of strategic management so that in the cases that make the turning points in the law, the factual record was developed with the complexities and the opportunities of Supreme Court litigation in mind. I wasn't successful in every case, or even most cases, but there were a select few whose importance was undoubted—for example, in 1976 I argued for the federal government as *amicus curiae* (a friend of the court) in the *Gregg v. Georgia* case upholding the death penalty.

I also tried, unsuccessfully for the most part, to implement forms of vertical communication and set up a kind of a trip-wire system so that when large issues hit the trial stage we would know about it and would be able to say something about the kind of factual record we would like to see prepared. One of the big issues at the time was presidential impoundment—when the president decides not to spend money appropriated by the U.S. Congress—and I hoped to ease the Court into accepting impoundment by starting with a statutory issue and moving later on to a constitutional issue. I argued the statutory case and got my hat handed to me. The court was very unfriendly to the impoundment, particularly because Richard Nixon was the president at the moment. (As I slowly realized, the unspoken rule was that Nixon was not to win any cases. That's not to say that the office of the presidency did not win any cases, for it certainly did. But the closer any particular case got to Richard Nixon the person, the quicker it was rejected.)

The most important mission of the solicitor general, and the aspect of the job that interested me most, is the opportunity to assist the Supreme Court in the development of legal doctrine. The elaboration of principle that the Court undertakes is an enormously difficult task, seeking to create stability and continuity in the law in times of crises and changing values. This is an intellectual task of most monumental proportions, but I think the effort to accomplish it is alone what legitimates the Supreme Court's power to govern us all. If it is not an institution that can elaborate principle and adhere to it, its power tends to become to that extent less legitimate. It is the function of the solicitor general's office to attempt haltingly and as well as we can to assist the Court in doing that.

The solicitor general bears a special relationship to the Court. He owes it complete intellectual candor, even when that impairs his effectiveness as an advocate—a tradition of the office I endeavored to maintain. The Court and its function under our Constitution are far more important than a government victory in any given case. We live in extraordinarily troubled times, but our institutions and our laws were not devised only for the easy, sunny days. They were built to cope with trouble, and to be ready when trouble comes.

I like to think that it is no inadvertence that the solicitor general is the only officer of the Department of Justice required by statute to be "learned in the law." I used to annoy the more sober-sided by saying that if Richard Wagner had written an opera about the solicitor general, it would have been called "Der Meister Shyster."

For those who find their vocation in the law, the solicitor general position truly is a dream job, and is particularly pleasant in quiet times. I, however, was to hold the position in the most interesting of times.

Acting Attorney General Robert H. Bork announces that he has named Assistant Attorney Henry Petersen to take over the Watergate investigation and press the case "to a conclusion." He said Petersen will have "direct charge of the Watergate case and all related matters previously directed by Special Prosecutor Archibald Cox."

1

Getting the Job

WHEN I FIRST MET RICHARD NIXON, I could see in his expression the conviction that someone had blundered badly. Nixon was notorious for his dislike of Ivy League professors, although he staffed his administration with a number of them. Aside from that, I was wearing a beard, and a reddish one at that. He almost visibly recoiled at being confronted with this apparition resembling an antiwar protester.

I was never quite sure exactly why I was offered the job of solicitor general. After I received the offer I asked a number of well-connected Washingtonians how they thought it might have happened. Almost invariably, each said that he had been responsible for coordinating the offer. After a while, I decided that such inquiries were a useless enterprise. Looking back, it seems clear that none of them had much to do with it. It was my first experience of the maxim that victory has a thousand fathers. I had to wait a while before experiencing the other half of the maxim: defeat is an orphan.

I suspect my selection was due more to Nixon than anybody else. Perhaps it's well to say at the outset that I did not find Richard M. Nixon to be the ogre or the threat to our constitutional order painted by his liberal enemies. As I recall, a writer summarizing Nixon's career wrote that Nixon had been unpleasant and dishonest as a child. Pulitzer Prize–winning author Gary Wills, no friend of Nixon, refuted the claim. In doing extensive research for his book *Nixon Agonistes*, Wills found that the young Nixon had been a model child. It was the mature Nixon, according to Wills, who diminished himself in an effort to emulate tough and ruthless men like Lyndon Johnson and the Kennedys. Wills might have reflected that, unlike Johnson and the Kennedy family, Nixon had no reserves of liberal goodwill to see him through the tough patches. In any event, it was and is my opinion that other presidents' policies—past and present—pose a greater threat to constitutional government.

My first connection with Nixon, tangential at best, came with an article I wrote for *The New Republic* in favor of Nixon's candidacy during the primaries of 1968. *The New Republic* was running a series with someone endorsing each of the candidates in the primaries of both parties. My best friend and fellow Yale Law School professor Alexander Bickel asked me to write in favor of Nixon, I think, after he asked the editor-in-chief to choose me. I was an unknown Yale professor and had no particular affinity for Nixon, but I think I might have been the only Ivy League professor *The*

New Republic could find without a deep-seated moral abhorrence to him.[1]

I wrote the article from London, where I was on sabbatical with my family writing a book on antitrust law. Well before the time of laptops, I traveled with footlockers crammed with books and articles and Xeroxes so that I could work on writing the book from anywhere.

A quick aside—upon arriving in England, we stopped only briefly and then left for a drive through France, Italy, and Austria. On the return trip, the British customs officer eyed me suspiciously and asked what I did for a living. I tried to avoid acknowledging that I was a Yale professor. So I said I taught.

"What do you teach?"

"School." Gradually he trapped me so I had to confess I was a Yale law professor—a breed not too popular with the general population at the time.

Finally he said, "A Yale professor with a beard, that's worth a body search right there!" I talked him out of that, but he responded, "Well, if you turn out to be L. Ron Hubbard I'll be fired." (L. Ron Hubbard, a science-fiction writer and the founder of Scientology, was not allowed in the British Isles at the time.) I spent the next year writing *The Antitrust Paradox*, which I finished upon returning to the United States, but didn't publish it until after 1978, after I left the solicitor general post.

In any case, the article must have come to the attention of someone in the campaign, because after Nixon was elected I received an invitation to the inauguration and inauguration balls, even though I had no connection with any of the people involved in the administration at that time. I remember the postman in London coming to the door rather wide-eyed as he delivered those official-looking envelopes from the White House.

I didn't hear again from the Nixon administration until I was approached by a couple of different headhunters after his reelection in 1972. One of them wanted to know if I was interested in being head of the Civil Rights Division of the Department of Justice. Given what I had written on the subject, particularly an article in *The New Republic* opposing the 1964 Civil Rights Act (the product of a discussion with and academic challenge from my friend Alex Bickel, and a position I later retracted), the offer took me by surprise.

In the course of the conversation, the same fellow asked me what my attitude toward civil rights was, particularly the situation with regards to matters of race, and I said that I agreed with Pat Moynihan's sentiment that now was the time for "benign neglect." The man said that that was exactly what the administration wanted, but I convinced him that I was not the man to nominate for that position.

At a later time, I was approached again by the same headhunter who wanted to know if I was interested in being head of the Antitrust Division of the Department of Justice. I once more had to say that, given what I had written, and believing much of modern antitrust law to be counterproductive and intellectually incoherent, I would have a terrible time being confirmed for that position.

My one direct encounter with President Nixon and his

administration before being offered the position of solicitor general came in the spring of 1972. I got a call from Roger Cramton, a friend and former dean of the Cornell University Law School who was then assistant attorney general in charge of the Office of Legal Counsel (OLC) in the Justice Department. The OLC, an office perhaps less well known than that of the solicitor general, provides legal advice to the attorney general and the White House, and is often considered a stepping-stone for the Supreme Court (Chief Justice Rehnquist was head of the Office of Legal Counsel immediately prior to his appointment to the Supreme Court, and Justice Scalia served in that post during the Ford administration).

I sensed the disappointment in his voice right away. The purpose of his call was to let me know that Richard Kleindienst, President Nixon's new attorney general, wanted me at the White House to help them find a way out of a predicament. During the course of the call, Roger also let slip that he thought he was going to be fired soon, a suspicion that proved true. (Allegedly, some in the White House considered him "too arrogant and outspoken"; they chalked up his resignation to "an eager desire to return immediately to teaching," even though it was the middle of the school year.)[2]

The issue at hand was a bill limiting the busing of school children. Nixon was coming up for reelection, and school busing was a hot topic in many communities. Nixon's aim was not to abolish busing, but to make it a more narrowly focused remedy and to abolish the excesses devised by various federal judges. Upon arriving in Washington in March 1972 and taking up offices in the New Executive Office Building, I discovered I was to work with Charles Alan Wright, a well-respected and influential law professor from the University of Texas. It was the first time I worked with Wright, but it wouldn't be the last.

We worked on the bill for most of a week. A majority of the final product was Wright's work, and I liked very little of it. The bill was, nevertheless, submitted to Nixon and his Cabinet Committee on Education. A meeting with the president was scheduled for Saturday of that week, and it was only then that Wright and I discovered that three partners from the law firm Kirkland & Ellis—Hammond Chaffetz, William Jentes, and Fred Bartlit—had been assigned by the White House to work on the same problem separately. Also in the meeting were some cabinet members, notably Attorney General Kleindienst and Secretary of Labor George Shultz, along with a crowd of staffers.

Unsure where to sit, I assumed the president would take a position at the end of the long table and I therefore sat near the middle of the table with my back to the windows. I was somewhat embarrassed when I discovered that I had taken the seat one away from Nixon with nobody between us. When the president came into the room he was introduced to the new members of his administration, shaking hands with them along with the various administration officials and members of the White House staff whom he did know. The result was that I was the last person he came to. He looked at me for the first time and, as I mentioned earlier, as somebody said, "This is Professor Bork from Yale Law

School," I could see him visibly recoil a step or two. A red-bearded professor from Yale struck him, I think, as a terrible anomaly in his administration.

The discussion of the draft bill went around the table clockwise but proved disappointing. When called upon, Kirkland & Ellis partner Hammond Chaffetz resorted to the old saw that "The important consideration for a litigator was the fact." Since we were discussing the constitutionality of a known set of facts, the observation did not prove very helpful.

Time and again, I have found the practitioner's view-point on the law to be of seriously limited use. As I think about it now, the professor's outlook is superior in at least one sense for the position of solicitor general, or would be so if professors could shed their absorption with ideology. The practitioner concentrates on one little aspect of the law at a time, trying to fit the facts into it, whereas the professor deals with more law more generally and abstractly. The practitioner becomes intimately familiar with a narrow range of issues, while the professor has a broader view. This is due not to the superior virtue of one approach or the other but to the requirements of their respective tasks.

Law is inescapably centered on the actual decisions rendered by the courts, but studying outside perspectives on those decisions is of far more practical importance than studying the underlying subject matter. For the past half-century, the political scientists and historians, not the lawyers, have produced the most interesting reflections on the Constitution. If you want, for example, to know the actual meaning of the religion clauses in the First Amendment, you are much better served to read scholars such as Walter Berns and Philip Hamburger—a political scientist and a legal historian, respectively—rather than the antihistorical opinions of the courts. The fact that most law schools now provide scant education in the law outside its practicality makes it increasingly difficult to take law seriously as an intellectual pursuit. Intellectual development requires reading material above one's own level, not below.

In any case, the professor has a decided advantage in dealing with the scope of issues that hit the desks of those working in the White House, and the busing bill was such a case. So when Chaffetz—a practitioner at heart, a first-rate one to be sure, but a practitioner all the same—lapsed into platitudes, it can likely be explained by his sudden realization that, probably for the first time in his life, he was being called upon to advise someone on an issue of constitutional theory, and that person just happened to be the president of the United States.

A feature of the draft bill I did not like was that it would give Congress authority to expand its control over the nation's school districts. The theory was that liberals could be bought off with that expansion of their authority and would, in return, allow restrictions on the amount of busing school districts could order. Aside from the dubious assumption that liberals could be bought off in this fashion and would not simply press for even more control of the schools, there was the difficulty that the tactic rested upon the assumption that Congress could control the substance of the Equal

Protection Clause by statute, an assumption that runs contrary to our entire constitutional history.

I was the last to speak as someone—I think it was George Shultz—asked me what I thought. I said that if the asserted power could rest only upon the Supreme Court precedent of *Katzenbach v. Morgan*, it would be resting on corrupt constitutional law, upon which this administration should not rely.

(In *Katzenbach v. Morgan*, the Court essentially concluded that Congress could control the meaning of the Equal Protection Clause so long as each successive interpretation resulted in more, and not less, equality. The objection had been raised that Congress was being given complete control over the Constitution, but the majority, in an opinion by William Brennan, replied that Congress could expand the meaning of equality under the Constitution, but would not be allowed to shrink it. The power being created by court order was thus a one-way ratchet moving always in the direction of more liberal control.)

Nixon gave a quick shake of his head, perhaps needing an extra second to reconcile the eminently reasonable opinion he had just heard with its proximity to the unreasonably bright red beard from whence it came, and responded, "I believe the same thing, but I didn't know there was a law professor anywhere in the United States who agreed with me." Our exchange did not evoke any strong response from any of the other lawyers in the room—practitioners, mostly. But I was pleasantly surprised to discover that Nixon's working knowledge of the law combined the virtues of the practitioner and the professor. When I spoke of *Katzenbach*, Nixon was surely at home with the discussion; the practitioners, however skilled, were not. In any case, I cannot be sure, but that may have been the moment when I got the job of solicitor general.

The meeting continued, and later a smaller group of us went into the Oval Office, where Nixon gave each outsider an inexpensive set of presidential cuff links. He explained the poor quality of the cuff links on the grounds that he wore the same ones, and that whenever he was in a crowd or riding in an open car people snatched the cuff links from his shirt, so he now used only cuff links he did not mind losing.

The final bill was worked out by Nixon on his famous yellow pad, and bore little resemblance either to Charles Alan Wright's bill or to my suggestions. The bill made a small stir when it was introduced, but ultimately died in Congress.

After that I did not hear again from anyone in the administration for several months. In the meantime, Nixon won reelection in a landslide over George McGovern. On Election Day I got calls from my Jewish Democrat friend Alex Bickel and my Irish Catholic Democrat friend Dennis Garvey, who both told me that for the first time in their lives they had voted Republican. With that, I knew it was all over but the counting.

It was a cold December afternoon in New Haven when I returned home from teaching a class at Yale Law School to find my second son, Charles, and my daughter, Ellen, sitting in my study in two chairs facing a television set on the floor. They were watching *The Avengers,* a popular program designed as a spoof of the James Bond movies. There was no other place for me to sit, so I took a seat on the floor between them and got a perfunctory greeting as they kept their eyes glued to the television. We'd been watching together for several minutes when the phone rang. The familiar tone must have registered just enough for Charles as, eyes still glued to the television, he casually relayed a message as I went to pick up the phone: "Oh, yeah—some general has been calling all day asking for you."

The "general" was U.S. Attorney General Richard Kleindienst. He asked if I would accept the position of solicitor general if it were offered. (It is customary to ask that question before offering anybody a job, as no president wants to be embarrassed by making an offer that is then rejected.) I replied that I most certainly would. When we hung up, I understood that I would be offered the job. My wife, Claire, was out of town on a college search with our older son, Robert, so I could not discuss the matter with her immediately. Instead, I invited my best friend and his wife, Alex and Joanne Bickel, to come to the house so I could tell them about it.

They arrived an hour or so later, and I had barely finished telling them the news before White House Counsel John Dean called. He asked me to come down to Camp David the next day to interview with the president. At first I told him I couldn't make it because I needed to take care of my children while Claire was out of town, but the Bickels overheard me and called out that they would take care of the kids, so I agreed to go. The only other memorable part of the conversation was Dean asking me, with a confidential chuckle, whether I had any skeletons in my closet. I said no, little knowing that if I had need of a skeleton I could borrow one from Dean's closet, which was overflowing with them.

Six months earlier, in June 1972, five men had been arrested while trying to bug the offices of the Democratic National Committee at the Watergate hotel and office complex in Washington, D.C., setting in motion the gears that would ultimately be President Nixon's undoing. Dean had been involved in devising the scheme and, by the time he called me in December, was well on his way to earning the title given to him by the FBI of "master manipulator of the Watergate cover-up."[3]

And so on the next morning, December 8, 1972, I went to the New Haven Airport to fly to Washington, D.C. As luck would have it, the plane was delayed long enough that I missed the helicopter at the Pentagon that was to take me to Camp David—a locale I affectionately refer to as "The Fuehrer Bunker"—so I was driven there by government car. When we arrived, the driver directed me to one of the smaller cabins, where I waited for a further summons. After a while the driver returned to take me to the president's cabin. It was snowing and extremely icy, and I remember walking from the car to the president's cabin worried that I would slip and suffer the indignity of meeting the president covered in snow.

President Nixon was perfectly pleasant, as he always was when I dealt with him. Apparently unsure if he was really dealing with a conservative Ivy League professor, he assured me his conservatism was something of a pose to keep others from moving too far left. I managed not to say that I would be happier if he were more conservative than he sounded.

We also discussed a little foreign policy: He described his trip to China, and I remember him saying that one of his strategies was to be somewhat unpredictable because it kept people who might be adversaries off balance, unsure of what he would do next. Perhaps the "Christmas Bombings" of North Vietnam he announced only a few days after our meeting were part of the same strategy—those surprised everybody.

It's possible that Nixon was contemplating the possibility of eventually elevating me to the Supreme Court, as most of our conversation consisted of a lecture by him on the duties of a judge. He went on for twenty or thirty minutes, and I was impressed because it was a very good lecture. I thought I could have given a slightly better one, but then I had been studying and teaching constitutional law for years, while Nixon had to be conversant not merely in judicial philosophy, but in a wide range of domestic and foreign affairs.

Nixon asked how old I was. When I said "Forty-five," he responded with a chipper "Perfect." I assume he wanted somebody who would be around a while, but who was old enough to be reasonably fixed in his views. Then he said it was just too bad I had gone to Yale. I rejoined that I hadn't gone to Yale, but to the University of Chicago. "That's almost as bad," he replied.

Many people have suggested that Nixon's deep-seated dislike of the Ivy League dated back to his early days out of Duke Law School. Though he graduated among the top of his class, he could not get a job offer from Wall Street, which tended to regard anything but Harvard, Yale, and Columbia as jerkwater schools. At the time Nixon graduated from Duke, Wall Street probably wasn't interested in hiring Chicago graduates, either. In any event, it seemed to have left quite a mark on him.

We then chatted briefly about his participation in the dedication of the new law school building at Chicago, a dramatic glass structure designed by the famous Finnish American architect Eero Saarinen, most famous for designing the Gateway Arch in St. Louis. We both marveled at how the place had escaped destruction at the hands of students during the Chicago riots.

He told me that Joseph Sneed, who was then dean of Duke Law School, would become the deputy attorney general, adding that "Politicians have had their turn in the Justice Department, and now it's the professors' turn." With that, our conversation came to an end; I was still no wiser about why I'd been chosen to be solicitor general.

Reaction to my nomination was decidedly mixed among the Yale faculty. Fellow law professor Thomas Emerson, for example, stopped me in the hallway and said, "I congratulate you, but not the country." I took it with a grain of salt. Emerson was known to generations of Yale Law students as Tommy the Commie. Ralph Winter, another Yale faculty member and a good friend, was fond of saying that when it came to Emerson, "Stupidity and lack of principle are racing neck and neck."

Another professor made it a point to say the following in a hallway conversation just loud enough so that I might hear: "It's the shame of the Law School that we have two Republicans on the faculty and other departments have none." He was wrong about that, since we had an incipient Republican among the twenty or thirty members of the faculty. And there were probably others at the university who were not identified as such because they kept their heads down.

Not all the responses were entirely hostile. Many thought it was funny. In my seminar course, a group of students presented me with a hard hat emblazoned with the solicitor general's logo on the front. They intended the joke to be that the position would take all the emotional and intellectual stamina of a construction foreman. The hard hat as protection against all the political debris cascading down in my first few months as solicitor general would prove a more apt metaphor.

Confirmation hearings for the position of solicitor general were scheduled for January 1973, even though the president had not begun his second term. The confirmation hearing was a fairly routine affair. When Democratic Senator Philip Hart from Michigan asked what he thought would be a trap question on my antitrust views, which were far different from the standard antitrust views of the time, I replied that I would enforce the administration's antitrust policy and not my own, and would apply the same position equally to other fields of law.

I was making a distinction between different views of the solicitor general's function: whether he is a lawyer for the government or an independent policy maker. I took the position that the solicitor general is a lawyer for the government. If he assumes an independent policy role, the government may have no means of presenting its views to the Court, thus crippling the administration's ability to make political choices even where there is no legal constraint on such choices.

Hart, with no choice but to accept my reasonable response, replied, "Well, that wipes out about twenty of my questions." Later I saw that none of this encounter appeared in the printed version of the hearings. As I learned, the senators can, and often do, revise their remarks to eliminate misstatements or anything potentially embarrassing to them. While that particular exchange wasn't much of an embarrassment, it was cut out.

Nixon's second inauguration on January 20, 1973, was the usual jubilant affair, with the president and first lady riding in an open car and marching bands from around the nation going down Pennsylvania Avenue from the Capitol to the White House. Claire and I came down from New Haven for the occasion, which included a reception in the White House.

It was Claire's first glimpse of Washington's version of

"nobility," and my first view of White House personnel celebrating rather than working. When we approached President Nixon in the receiving line, he leaned over the line to say into my ear, "Go give 'em Hell in the Supreme Court."

Of more interest, in retrospect, was the presence in the receiving line of Vice President Agnew. When I met him in the line, Agnew displayed considerable attention to me. In a remark unusual for a vice president to make to a solicitor general (whose duties did not ordinarily intersect with the vice president) let alone a solicitor general-in-waiting (as I would not assume the position until June), he said he wanted to have a meeting with me and would have his office offer a date once I moved to Washington and settled into my new position that June. Though I did not realize it at the time (nor did he, most likely), Agnew's political fortunes were beginning a death spiral.

Erwin Griswold, the former dean of Harvard Law School, was my immediate predecessor as solicitor general. Nixon wanted to get rid of Griswold, but he was reluctant to fire him outright; so the White House announced, without notifying Griswold in advance, that he had chosen to retire and that I would be his replacement.

Griswold asked me to let him stay on until the end of the Supreme Court's term, and I agreed. I had no particular wish to rush him out of office, but I remember one of the senators mentioning during my confirmation hearings that he didn't feel comfortable with the idea of confirming people so far ahead of their taking office.

In any event, I arranged with Griswold that I would come

down once a week or so to familiarize myself with the job. There was a small alcove-like office right off the main office of the solicitor general where I sat. It turned out there was very little to learn: the basic job was the practice of law, and I had practiced law, so I was not being plunged into something I didn't understand.

Although the times I did go down felt a bit like a waste, had I gone more often, I probably would have had a much better sense of how the Watergate scandal was creeping its way closer and closer to the White House. Richard Kleindienst, who replaced John Mitchell as attorney general a mere five days before the time of the Watergate break-in (coordinated and approved in large part by Mitchell), never received the trust or respect from the White House he deserved. I suspect his refusal of coconspirator G. Gordon Liddy's request that he release the burglars, though wise, soured him to the White House staff. Kleindienst was always very popular inside the Justice Department, and unflinchingly loyal. Yet for some reason the White House had him pigeonholed as an "unreliable hip shooter, not to be trusted on matters of policy or personnel."[4]

I happened to be in Washington on the day Kleindienst announced that he had been asked by the president to resign. At the same time, Nixon had also requested the resignation of two of his aides, Harry Robbins "Bob" Haldeman and John Ehrlichman, who, along with Dean and Mitchell, were deeply involved in the Watergate scandal.

During my weekly visits I got a taste of what might have been had Haldeman and Ehrlichman stuck around.

Ehrlichman was an assistant to the Cabinet Committee on Education, whose work on the busing bill had brought me to Washington in the first place. In that position he was a charming man, but when I saw him again as a member of the executive branch, he seemed to think I owed him some particular loyalty. Whenever I saw him he lifted his chin, giving me a Caesar-like profile.

As for Haldeman, I never met the man, but one aide captured Haldeman's essence in a brief encounter from the campaign trail: When the assistant was leaving a hotel and making his way across the parking lot, Haldeman appeared from a room balcony overlooking the lot and captured the attention of the young man by shouting, "Halt, aide!"

The White House did Kleindienst a final disservice by announcing his resignation alongside those of Ehrlichman and Haldeman (who were always particularly wicked to Kleindienst) and the firing of John Dean—tacitly implicating him in the Watergate scandal even though he had no real involvement. When Kleindienst told the staff, Henry Petersen, then head of the Criminal Division, gave quite an emotional speech about how unfair this timing was to Kleindienst.

Now obligated to nominate Kleindienst's successor, Nixon chose Elliot Richardson, who was then secretary of defense and probably would have preferred to remain in that position. The confirmation process offered Congress an irresistible opportunity to play politics. The Senate Judiciary Committee made Richardson's confirmation contingent upon his appointment of a special prosecutor satisfactory to the Senate. It was an astonishingly belittling moment as the entire Department of Justice was held hostage by the Committee until its new leader admitted it was essentially incapable of performing its function when it came to Watergate. It was a serious blow to Department morale. Many officials considered leaving, but feared the timing of their departure would be taken as complicity in the Watergate scandal.

Under great pressure, Richardson chose his old law school professor Archibald Cox. This was a particularly unfortunate choice; Cox was a man of integrity, but he was the protégé of Senator Edward Kennedy—Nixon's bitterest enemy—and closely allied with the entire Kennedy family.

To make matters worse, Griswold, still stinging from the way the White House chose to relieve him of his duties as solicitor general, offered his office in the Department of Justice building for the swearing in of Cox. Sure enough, Ted Kennedy and Ethel Kennedy, the widow of Robert Kennedy, were prominent members of the small audience invited to the investiture. The flaunting of his Kennedy connection at the swearing-in increased Nixon's already strong paranoia. Nixon came to see Cox's appointment as destined to undercut the White House. Perhaps inviting the Kennedys was just a lapse in judgment on Cox's part. But I doubt it.

In any case, Richardson assumed the position of attorney general in late May, and had been in position for only a few weeks when he hired William Ruckelshaus, who had just lost an election bid to the U.S. Senate, to be the deputy attorney general. Hiring Ruckelshaus took some adroitness on Richardson's part (Kleindienst had tried and failed to appoint Ruckelshaus on three separate occasions), particularly because Joe Sneed had been deputy attorney general for only a short time. Nixon, a fellow Duke Law School graduate, would not simply dismiss Sneed. Richardson suggested to Nixon that he nominate Sneed for a vacancy on the Ninth Circuit Court of Appeals, a position Nixon was happy to offer to Sneed, and Sneed happy to accept.

My adventures in Washington had an ominous prelude. A few weeks before I was to be sworn in and officially start the job as solicitor general, I took the family to stay at a friend's cottage at Rehoboth Beach for a couple of days. I went swimming while the rest of the family stayed on the beach. Unfamiliar with ocean swimming, I was caught in an outgoing current and began to be pulled out to sea. I waved my arms frantically to get help from the family. They mistook the gesture, however, and waved back, grinning in a jovial mood. I extricated myself from the outgoing current, swam back to shore, and rejoined the family, not without recriminations. It is not a pleasant sensation to have one's frantic gestures for help interpreted as expressions of joy as one faces the prospect of never returning. My family, however, remained unmoved.

On June 26, Richardson presided in the attorney general's conference room as I was sworn into office by Chief Justice Warren Burger before a gathering of perhaps forty or fifty officials from the Department. As is customary, my children were present, and my wife, Claire, held the Bible used to administer the oath.

I was on top of the world. The solicitor general's job is a real plum. I came aboard with high hopes for the Nixon administration, knowing we had a very good team assembled in the Justice Department—people with an intellectual appreciation of the law. Watergate had happened, but it was not yet big news. I had no inkling of what was to befall me in the next six months. I did believe, long after it was reasonable to do so, that President Nixon could not have been so careless as to have gotten caught up in what events later showed he had been.

2

Nixon's Defense Attorney Offer

SPIRO AGNEW DID NOT particularly impress me in his public life as attack dog for the Nixon administration, but then I was not particularly impressed by most politicians. I certainly preferred Agnew to the liberal Democrats who controlled Congress, the courts, and the bureaucracies. I also enjoyed Agnew's wildly colorful phrases, written for him by William Safire, such as his description of liberals as "nattering nabobs of negativism." I had no idea, however, whether I would prefer Agnew to others seeking the Republican nomination. Be that as it may, we scheduled a meeting a few days after I started the solicitor general job, and I went to Agnew's office at the appointed time prepared to hear something of interest.

I was quite surprised, therefore, after having been ushered into Agnew's office, to discover that he really had nothing of substance to say. I was expecting some sort of conversation about his future run for the presidency, but instead the conversation was desultory, leading nowhere. After about twenty minutes an aide came in with a photograph that had been taken at the beginning of our visit. This marked the end of our conversation, and I returned to my office at the Department of Justice rather confused about the whole episode.

A few weeks after my meeting with Agnew, I was sitting in my office reviewing the briefs for the upcoming fall term in the Supreme Court when I got a call from White House Chief of Staff Alexander Haig. He asked me how late I worked. I replied that I would probably be going home around 6:30 or 7:00, and he asked if I would mind dropping by the White House to see him that evening. He didn't tell me why, and I didn't quite understand it, but I went to meet him nonetheless.

As it turned out, Haig had an offer to make. He asked me to become Nixon's chief defense counsel. On July 16, 1973, former White House Deputy Assistant Alexander Butterfield had appeared before the Senate Select Committee to Investigate Campaign Practices (the Senate Watergate Committee) and revealed the existence of a secret taping system that Nixon had installed in the White House, telling the Committee members that all conversations in the White House at which Nixon was present were recorded. With this revelation, the need for Nixon to augment his personal legal team became obvious.

Haig told me that Nixon already had a number of lawyers, but nobody was in charge and the operation was not running well. For example, nobody on the legal team had any idea that Butterfield was going to disclose the existence of a White House taping system during his testimony. They badly needed somebody to take charge of the defense.

Haig was very persuasive. He talked about the mess the defense was in. He also talked about the fact that somebody in the White House was leaking internal memoranda to a high-up officer in the Navy, which Haig referred to as "military penetration of the White House."

It was at this point that Haig told me Vice President Agnew was under investigation for accepting bribes in exchange for construction contracts granted while he was governor of Maryland, which was news to me. The investigation, conducted by U.S. Attorney Griffin Bell in Baltimore, had been going on for several months. By the time I heard about it, there was even some question about whether Agnew continued receiving kickbacks while vice president (he had).

The missing pieces of my conversation with Agnew a few weeks earlier fell into place. It's my estimation that Agnew was already starting to think about putting a team together for his future presidential run when he first asked to meet with me at the inauguration in January. By the time I assumed the position of solicitor general and we could arrange a meeting, Agnew must have known the chickens from his kickback scheme were finally coming home to roost, and his presidential hopes were dashed. He had the good grace not to cancel our meeting, which had been arranged under the pretense of a meet and greet anyhow.

In any event, Haig had me 90 percent convinced that I would resign as solicitor general and take over the job as chief defense counsel for President Nixon. He was great at waving the flag and telling you the republic depended on you.

I went home to give the proposition more thought away from the pressures of the White House, and once again turned to my good friend Alex Bickel. I called his home in New Haven, and his wife told me he happened to be nearby, staying at the Hay-Adams in Washington. So I called the Hay-Adams and asked him to come out to my home in McLean, Virginia, disclosing only that I needed his advice on a sensitive topic. He told me he would find a cab and head straight over. I waited forever, it seemed, and finally got a call from Bickel saying he was back at the hotel because the cab couldn't find the place. He suggested it could wait and we would talk some other time, but I was persistent—I had to talk to him that night. So again he grabbed a taxi, and this time I had Claire drive out with me to meet him on the main road. We collected Bickel and turned around to head home. When we reached our street, Turkey Run Road, I suggested that Claire stop the car so Bickel and I could get out and walk the dark, semi-rural road home. It's an indication of the paranoia of the time that I really wanted to be someplace where it was impossible to be overheard.

Claire drove the car back to the house, and as Bickel and I walked, I explained to him what I had been offered, and Haig's persuasive pitch. The paranoia subsided by the time we reached the house, and we continued the conversation and drank well into the morning. Once I had the chance to cool off and discuss it with Alex—whose judgment I always valued (especially when he agreed with me)—I realized it was a job I did not want. In the morning, not in the best shape, I dropped by Elliot Richardson's home in a nearby neighborhood and we discussed it. He also thought there were several hang-ups: for example, the difficulties of not being able to operate with all the freedom of a private attorney.

The time came to see Haig. Considering my condition from the past night's drinking, I am to this day unsure how I managed to deliver one of the best oral arguments of my life, convincing Haig it was a bad idea for him to hire me.

I began by asking him how I would be paid.

"Well, you'll be on government payroll," he responded.

"Well, that raises a problem," I replied, "because if I'm a government attorney, I am not like the usual defense attorney who, if he comes across material damaging to his client, can simply sit on it without handing it over. As a government attorney, sworn to uphold the law and so forth, I would be required if I came across damaging information to turn it over to the U.S. Attorney's Office."

It seemed to me that with that remark, the ardor to have me become the chief defense counsel started to cool.

I also asked how people would know that I was in charge. Would I have a title?

He chuckled and said no, but I would be the only one who would have access to the president, which would indicate that I was in charge.

"That's fine, but if the time comes when I have to give some advice that isn't wanted, I'll be sitting by a telephone that never rings."

"Very perceptive of you," Haig replied.

Finally, able to ignore the elephant in the room no longer, I said, "And, of course, I'll have to hear the tapes."

Haig wasted no time in his reply: "You can't hear the tapes. This president feels so strongly about the executive privilege of the office of the presidency that if he is ever forced to turn over those tapes he will burn them first, and then resign."

At that point there came to my mind the best sentence I never spoke. I began to say, "If that's true, why doesn't he burn them now?" Then I had a vision of a White House aide burning the tapes in the Rose Garden, and saying he was doing this on the advice of the solicitor general. I held my tongue.

By the end of the conversation, I had Haig convinced I was not the man for the job. And so I returned to my post in the solicitor general's office. A few weeks later I got a phone call from Nixon, which admittedly was not about much, and thus seemed out of place. As my wife astutely noted, it was his way of telling me that the fact that I had turned down the job was all right; he didn't hold it against me.

3

William O. Douglas's War

THE FIRST MAJOR EVENT of my term as solicitor general was the United States military incursion into Cambodia. Before I tell the tale of my legal battle with Justice William O. Douglas over the Cambodia bombing, a few words about my relationship with Douglas both before and after these events will help put everything in context.

Douglas was a man I had difficulty fathoming. For example, A. Raymond "Ray" Randolph, a brilliant young lawyer in the office, was once arguing a case before the Court. The justices, as sometimes happens, lost interest and began whispering among themselves. Douglas, however, sitting toward the center of the Court, was writing furiously and looking up from time to time at Ray as he wrote. Ray concluded that only Douglas was paying attention and directed his argument entirely to him. As he finished his argument, Ray looked at Douglas, who picked up an envelope, licked the seal, and closed it; Douglas had been doing his correspondence during the argument. It was not the only time Douglas played this mildly cruel trick on a lawyer.

But there was another side to Douglas. I once was in the Supreme Court, sitting directly before the bench, when a page appeared and handed me a piece of notepaper. Written on it was a message that the sender wished to host a luncheon for me at the Court, and that other attendees of the party would be the members of the Court. I couldn't make out the name from the signature, however, nor were there any stationery markings. When the Court left the chamber I asked the clerk whose signature it was. To my amazement, he said it was William O. Douglas. My views on the law were quite different from Douglas's, and I had spilled a fair amount of ink criticizing him in particular, so the invitation was wholly unexpected. If I had been asked to guess who had issued me such an invitation, I probably would have named every other member of the Court before Douglas.

On the appointed day, I went to the justices' dining room at the Court, where a bartender tended a small portable bar. I was the first to arrive, and a few minutes later Douglas came in. "There is no business purpose to this meeting," he told me. "It's just to show you that you have friends in this town." The other justices came in shortly afterward. When the lunch was over, Douglas waited until the others had left and then repeated his statement that the lunch had no business purpose, but was merely to show me that I had friends in Washington.

This softened my view of Douglas, but by no means dispelled the enigma of his personality. A few months after the luncheon at the Supreme Court, Douglas and I and our wives were at the annual banquet of the antitrust bar and, as is the custom, Douglas and my wife sat side by side to the left of the podium while I sat next to Mrs. Douglas on the right side of the podium. For some reason my wife and Douglas began to discuss the Yale Law School, where Douglas had once taught. He said that Yale was intellectually dead, and that nothing was taking place there. My wife protested, naming work being undertaken by a number of the faculty, including Alex Bickel.

"Alex Bickel is a whore," Douglas barked. The fact that Douglas knew that Bickel was my best friend and also knew that Bickel was even then dying of cancer made the remark all the more ghastly.

My wife, taken aback, said, "Why would you say a thing like that?"

Douglas replied, "I don't propose to waste a perfectly good evening in Washington trying to explain something to a lady who could not conceivably understand."

My wife picked up her chair and turned it sideways to look at the entertainment at the end of the hall and put her back to Douglas. He tried repeatedly to get her attention, whispering, "Your husband has integrity."

At that point, Judge Malcolm Wilkey, seated next to Claire on the other side, asked what was wrong, to which my wife replied, "I have just been horribly insulted."

"Pay no attention to the old bastard," Wilkey advised.

Now to the episode at hand, one that illustrates the inanity of attempting to make military decisions in a courtroom. It also throws light upon Justice Douglas's judicial philosophy.

I had taken up my duties as solicitor general less than five weeks earlier, barely enough time to familiarize myself with the rest of the lawyers in the office. I was sitting in my office admiring the Art Deco woodwork and handsome shelves, replete with Supreme Court opinions, when my complacency was suddenly shattered. Justice Douglas, vacationing at his home in Goose Prairie in the state of Washington, had issued an order on Saturday, August 4, for the United States to cease bombing in support of operations in Cambodia.

The legal, procedural, and military messes created by judges attempting to displace military judgment in wartime are illustrated by various judicial reactions to America's incursion into Cambodia during the Vietnam War. Antiwar groups such as the American Civil Liberties Union (ACLU), determined to achieve a result in the courts they could not achieve in Congress, had filed suit to enjoin United States military operations in Cambodia.

The United States military incursion into Cambodia was designed to reduce the fighting capabilities of the North Vietnamese troops who were using Cambodia as a safe haven for attacks across the border on U.S. troops. The incursion was the subject of a heated political battle in the United States between pro- and antiwar factions. The political branches of the United States Congress ultimately resolved the controversy democratically, specifying August 15, 1973, as the date United States operations in and over Cambodia had to cease.

The case began when antiwar groups filed a complaint in a federal district court in Manhattan seeking an order to stop military operations in and over Cambodia. A little background on the episode will prove informative here.

In response to the North Vietnamese use of eastern Cambodia as a base point from which to attack South Vietnam, President Nixon ordered the Air Force to begin a campaign of bombing in Cambodia. By mid-1973 there was significant opposition in Congress to any U.S. military activity in Cambodia. That opposition culminated in a provision in the July 1, 1973, appropriations bill, which would cut off funds for all operations in Cambodia by August 15, 1973.[1] Before that political resolution was worked out, the ACLU brought suit in an attempt to stop the bombing in Cambodia.

Filing a suit in federal court to try to stop the Vietnam War was a popular tactic with antiwar groups like the ACLU,[2] and their first temporary victory came in this attempt to stop the Cambodia bombing. In April 1973, the ACLU recruited Congresswoman Elizabeth Holtzman, a Democrat from New York, along with four Air Force officers, to file suit against Secretary of Defense James Schlesinger and others in the United States District Court for the Eastern District of New York. Holtzman argued that the bombing in Cambodia lacked congressional authorization and was therefore unconstitutional. The government argued that the bombing was part of the larger war in Vietnam. As such, it was a tactical decision, one the president was entitled to make.

Like other legal challenges during the Vietnam War, *Holtzman v. Schlesinger* was handled by the U.S. Attorney's Office in the district in which it was brought. A case like this, which the government would presume is not meritorious, is not generally managed by the Department of Justice or the solicitor general's office at the district court level. The plaintiffs sought relief in the form of an injunction to prevent bombing in Cambodia.

The district court judge ruled in the ACLU's favor on July 25, 1973, but delayed the imposition of the injunction until 4:00 p.m. on July 27.[3] The judge concluded that "there is no Congressional authorization to fight in Cambodia after the withdrawal of American troops and the release of American prisoners of war" which was effectuated by the Paris Agreement of January 27, 1973.[4] On July 27 a three-judge panel of the Second Circuit heard argument and stayed the injunction pending appeal. (A stay is a judicial order postponing or halting a proceeding, judgment, or other order.)[5] At this point the solicitor general's office got involved.

In the midst of the procedural turmoil I received a call from Henry Kissinger, then–national security advisor, who assured me that running the Cambodian war was in no way a function of the judiciary. I agreed with him, of course, but pointed out that the problem was getting the courts to agree as well.

The only course open to the plaintiffs was to ask Thurgood Marshall, the justice for the Second Circuit, to lift the stay. Marshall held a hearing in Washington, D.C., on Wednesday, August 1, at which the solicitor general's office represented the government. Marshall, exercising judicial prudence, recognized that the Second Circuit had not abused its discretion in issuing the stay and that it "would exceed [his] judicial authority were [he], acting alone, to grant th[e] application" to lift the stay.[6]

Once the justice for a particular circuit rules on a stay, the applicants are free to go to any other justice they choose to seek a different outcome. In this case, they chose Justice Douglas, as I knew they would. Despite the assurance of my deputies that no justice would hear such a petition, Douglas nevertheless arranged an oral argument in the post office building of Yakima, Washington, a town near where he was spending the summer. Argument was held that Friday, August 3, with the government represented by attorneys I designated to make the argument.

As I had predicted, Justice Douglas lifted the stay the Second Circuit had placed on the order to stop military operations in Cambodia, and so that order went into effect. This was a particularly sharp judicial incursion into U.S. military operations and into a dispute between Congress and the president, especially considering that the agreed-upon end date for military actions in Cambodia was less than two weeks away.

Douglas's reasoning was, to put the matter no higher, distinctly peculiar. He asserted that the case was similar to a death penalty case. In death penalty cases a stay can be issued to provide time for the merits of an appeal to be addressed. Thus, Douglas argued, a stay could be issued here without addressing the merits because "denial of the application before me would catapult our airmen as well as Cambodian peasants into the death zone."[7] The difficulty with employing this reasoning is that, while a stay of execution merely holds the order in abeyance, an order directing military operations would not preserve the status quo but would alter outcomes on the battlefield. Furthermore, the gravity of the case was so great, Douglas said, he was required to ignore principles that would ordinarily decide the case in the government's favor.

Douglas displayed his penchant for allowing his personal views to cloud reasoned judgment and the rule of law. His entire approach to the matter was to view it as a capital case, rather than one in which the tactical operations of the United States military and the country's foreign policy were being litigated: "This case, in its stark realities, involves the grim consequences of a capital case . . . the present case involves whether Mr. X (an unknown person or persons) should die."[8] His concern for "Cambodian farmers whose only 'sin' is a desire for socialized medicine to alleviate the suffering of their families and neighbors"[9] led Douglas to determine that the Cambodia bombing campaign violated the Constitution. He offered no explanation as to why the farmer's view of socialized medicine, pro or con, had anything to do with the American incursion into Cambodia.

Douglas's assertion that "the upshot is that we know that someone is about to die" led him to conclude: "I see no reason to balance the equities and consider the harm to our foreign policy if one or a thousand more bombs do not drop."[10]

Despite his assurances that he would not judge the

legality of the war, Justice Douglas did just that when he ruled that the war violated Article I, Section 8, Clause 11, which confers upon Congress the power to "declare War," and which he believed confers exclusive power over war and peace upon Congress.

Douglas was not deterred by questions of justiciability, standing, or political question, doctrines that might have ended the case in the government's favor. Indeed, by Douglas's reasoning the United States could not conduct a war or engage in any use of force without a full-scale trial. Improbable as this may seem, some American judges wish to exercise just such a power.

The orders of Douglas and the district court judge were particularly egregious because Congress and the president had already worked out a timetable by which the bombing and other military operations in Cambodia would cease on August 15. The political branches of government had made a political judgment about war and peace, a judgment that should not have been interfered with by the judiciary.

At this point in the whole affair I was interrupted from my office daydream when a member of my staff appeared at my door and said the Defense Department wanted to know whether they could continue bombing despite Douglas's decision. I was about to respond, "Why don't they ask a lawyer?" before it hit me that they already had one, me. I mulled it over for no more than a few minutes, and was about to answer yes, when the same staff member came back in and said that Defense no longer wanted an opinion. I put this down to wariness from the Pentagon about receiving official counsel from a bearded Yale Law professor who might well be a peacenik. They need not have worried. Ultimately, the Pentagon would receive my opinion anyhow, since the federal government had to go to court to remedy what Douglas had done.

I needed to respond to Douglas's lifting of the stay, and fast. The only remaining avenue of redress for the United States was to petition Justice Marshall, the circuit justice for the Second Circuit, to impose his own stay of the district court's order. We petitioned Marshall for such relief immediately after hearing of Justice Douglas's lifting the Second Circuit's stay.

I had prepared for this move by obtaining an affidavit from Secretary of State William Rogers stating that a cease in bombing could cause grave damage to the United States by exposing our troops in the area, along with the villagers who sided with the United States in the war. The affidavit may have been crucial in persuading Marshall to impose his own stay and in securing the agreement of seven other justices with that stay.

The case was so clear that I, and others, became a trifle nervous at the delay in Justice Marshall's ruling. We had filed on the morning of August 4, yet by mid-afternoon we still had heard nothing. Finally, toward the end of the business day, the Court issued an order staying the district court's injunction order.[11] The cause of the delay was noble; Justice

Marshall had secured support for the stay from every other member of the Court other than Douglas.

Douglas took the unusual step of writing a dissent to Marshall's in-chambers issuance of a stay. His dissent was volcanic. He decried even the Court's decision to reverse his order lifting the stay as a violation of the Court's authority to act with a quorum:

> I am firmly convinced that the telephonic disposition of this grave and crucial constitutional issue is not permissible. . . . It is a matter of law and order involving high principles. The principles are that the Court is a deliberative body that acts only on reasoned bases after full consideration, and that it is as much bound by the law of the land as is he who lives in the ghetto or in the big white house on the hill.[12]

Justice Douglas was focusing on the statute that gives the Court its powers, which states, "The Supreme Court of the United States shall consist of a Chief Justice of the United States and eight associate justices, any six of whom shall constitute a quorum."[13] While an individual Justice may take certain actions, such as issuing a stay or a writ of habeas corpus, the Court's rules bind the justices to not overturn these actions without a quorum. Douglas's reasoning represents a stretch of the Court's rules and authorizing statute, and is directly contradicted by his own action in lifting the Second Circuit's stay. When he took this action he was, in effect, overturning Justice Marshall's prior decision not to do so.

Douglas's desire to direct the military during the Vietnam War led him in his dissent to decry fervently the Court's "seriatim telephone calls" which "cannot . . . be a lawful substitute" for a conference. If the Court's members, acting during a recess, choose to stay a lower court from infringing upon the domain of the political branches, neither the Constitution nor the rule of law is at risk. If, however, Justice Douglas, or federal district courts were left free to direct a war being fought on foreign soil, the constitutional distribution of power would be in peril.

Douglas's dissent missed the mark. Though a single justice may not overturn a ruling of the Court, it is clear that a single justice may issue a stay that another justice had declined to issue. In this case, Marshall alone issued a stay and seven other justices did no more than note their agreement with it.

The bombing proceeded and ended on the schedule for the withdrawal of our troops agreed to by the president and Congress. With a first major legal victory in hand, I expected to spend the autumn preparing for my first Supreme Court session as solicitor general. My first oral argument in front of the Supreme Court was less than two months away, and I hoped to be well prepared. It would not be long until I considered myself lucky to be prepared at all.

4

L'Affaire Agnew

Vice President Spiro T. Agnew first informed the White House that he was under investigation by a Maryland grand jury in April 1973, but he claimed not to be involved in a bribery scheme. Agnew asked if the White House could speak with Senator John Glenn Beall, Jr., brother of the U.S. attorney, "to alert him that the White House didn't want Agnew's name to come up in an unnecessary or embarrassing way."[1] President Nixon rightly declined to do so.

Upon being informed that Agnew was under investigation, Al Haig exhibited his sharp instincts, immediately recognizing the necessity of decoupling the vice president's case from Watergate to deal with them separately; "otherwise [the president and vice president would] go down together and the country [would] go with them."[2] Haig describes his initial reaction:

> In my own mind, two words formed: *double impeachment.* I am not subject to visions, but as [Attorney General Elliot] Richardson left my office a vivid picture grew in my mind of the president and vice president of the United States, both charged with high crimes and misdemeanors, side by side, on trial together before the Senate.[3]

Haig immediately contacted White House Special Counsel Fred Buzhardt to inquire about the possibility of a double impeachment. Buzhardt described the ordeal rather accurately, as a "coup d'etat with the legislative branch taking over the executive branch under the cover of the Constitution."[4] No one wanted the presidency to be passed to Carl Albert, the Democratic congressman from Oklahoma and then-speaker of the House, including Carl Albert himself, who reputedly was terrified of the idea.

Elliot Richardson continued looking into the allegations against Agnew. By July he concluded, "he had never seen such an open-and-shut case,"[5] finding Agnew indictable on more than forty felony counts.

By early August, the Agnew investigation was placing its strain on Nixon. In his memoirs, Nixon notes that he "objectively recognized the weight of Richardson's evidence, but emotionally I was still on Agnew's side. I wanted to believe him."[6] Nixon was caught in a dilemma: Either support Agnew, which would further diminish his credibility once the charges were substantiated, or abandon Agnew and lose the vice president's political base in the process. In light of

Agnew's public denials of all wrongdoing, Nixon chose the correct course, urging Haig to plant the idea of resignation in Agnew's mind.[7]

Agnew maintained his innocence, suggesting that Richardson wanted him out of the way so he could pursue the presidency. Nixon, concerned that Agnew be treated fairly, arranged for Henry Petersen, head of the Criminal Division, to conduct "his own independent investigation of the case and to prepare his own independent recommendation."[8] Nixon assured Agnew he could vouch for Petersen's thoroughness, fairness, and impartiality, an assessment with which I wholeheartedly agree. In mid-August, Petersen returned his conclusion that the case against Agnew was quite strong.[9]

Agnew remained adamant about his innocence. Never one to miss out on making a little extra cash—as we were discovering more and more by the day—Agnew also insisted that if the White House did force him out, he hoped to remain in the administration a few more months to ensure his pension would vest. Never were Agnew's monetary priorities cast in such high relief to those of Nixon, whose self-espoused first rule of a successful political career was "Never let a dollar touch your hand."

By that time, the question of what to do about Vice President Agnew was becoming a pressing matter for the Department of Justice. The Department had no experience dealing with a vice presidential criminal. Some suggested the issue was being blown out of proportion, and could be finessed by citing Agnew's vice presidency as giving him immunity from prosecution while he remained in office. Others, including myself, thought it was disgraceful to have a man taking bribes while vice president. Of course the point was not just that it was disgraceful—it would have been even more disgraceful to have a president engaged in such venality —but that the vice president's constitutional responsibilities were not such as to force an indefinite postponement of prosecution.

Richardson was torn, as well he might be, between those in the Department of Justice and the White House who did not want Agnew indicted, and those who felt he must be. I once asked him what he could say before a congressional committee when asked why he had not indicted Agnew. That had a clarifying effect, since there was no solid reason not to indict. I do not blame Richardson for his initial confused response because, though I did not know it, my time for confusion in a crisis was close. When the call came from the White House, Richardson had made up his mind and reached the correct conclusion, telling them we would have to indict Agnew.

Even though most in the White House realized Agnew would have to go, there was still some trepidation about the firestorm that the indictment would cause. I think they were hoping we at the Justice Department would drag our feet long enough to give Agnew a chance to resign first. By mid-August, they asked Richardson to come in for a meeting to discuss the matter further. He agreed, with the qualification that he would be able to bring me along as well.

When Richardson and I arrived for the meeting, among

those present were Haig, special counsels Fred Buzhardt and Leonard Garment (who had been Nixon's law partner in the sixties, and remains a more than competent clarinet player), and Charles Alan Wright (whom I had not seen since we worked on the busing bill together; he subsequently took the job as Nixon's defense attorney after I refused the offer).

We had a session in which it seemed clear that the White House personnel had been sent by the president to beat on us until we agreed to delay the indictment proceedings, if not suspend them all together.

For about an hour they argued vigorously with Elliot and me that now was not the time to indict Agnew. One of the arguments they made was that Agnew's political base was the same as the president's, and attacking Agnew would alienate part of that base from Nixon. At any rate, when it became clear that Richardson and I would not give way, Haig said, "Let's go see the president."

On our walk to the Oval Office, Richardson mentioned that he needed to use the bathroom. Sensing the unusual timing of the request, I followed suit and said that I could use a pit stop as well. My hunch was correct: as soon as the door to the men's room closed behind us, Richardson turned on all the faucets in the expectation that the noise of running water would make our conversation inaudible if anybody was eavesdropping electronically. Such was the atmosphere and the level of distrust in the White House. Though at the time it seemed a reasonable precaution, much like my walk along Turkey Run Road with Bickel about the job as Nixon's defense attorney, the whole thing had an air of low comedy about it.

Elliot, concerned that Nixon might order us to delay or suspend our proceedings, said, "I think this is a resignation issue, don't you?"

"I certainly do," I replied. Neither of us could see continuing with our jobs and ignoring a criminal in our midst.

Suggesting the possibility of one's resignation is a most delicate matter. It will not do to use the threat of resignation as a bludgeon to force a superior into a desired course of action. To open a discussion with that threat would force an executive with any backbone to call the bluff. On the other hand, to wait until a decision has practically been made before raising the question of resignation would also be ineffective in securing the reaction sought. It is probably best in most cases to leave the question of resignation unexpressed but lingering like a fragrance in the air. Richardson's instincts were similar to mine in this regard, and we agreed not to raise the issue of resignation directly, but rather to let our evident seriousness make it plain to Nixon that resignation was a strong possibility.

We left the restroom and continued to the Oval Office. From Nixon's perspective, Haig sat on the left side of Nixon's desk and Richardson on the right; before him and slightly to the right was Buzhardt, while I sat slightly center left. The discussion took the form of an almost formal debate, and Buzhardt and I did most of the debating, prompted by Nixon as he explored each issue. Buzhardt wasn't a particularly strong debater, as his primary duty for Nixon was "messaging."

It was said of Buzhardt that he was such a master manipulator of the press, he could leak a story to the publication of his choosing simply by handing the story to the correct mailroom clerk as he passed by. As Richardson once recalled from a conversation with someone in the Pentagon, "If you ever need a job done with no traces, Fred Buzhardt is your man. He can bury a body six feet deep without turning a shovelful of dirt."[10]

My main point was that nothing was to be gained by avoiding a confrontation with Agnew. The U.S. attorney in Baltimore was going ahead with trials of those who had bribed Agnew, which meant that Agnew's name and picture would be on the front pages of newspapers for months to come. The damage to the administration would be quite as great as if Agnew himself had been indicted. In fact, it would be worse, because, in addition to Agnew's guilt being shown, our refusal to indict him would make it look as though the president were covering up a crime within his own administration. The decision must be made, and made rapidly, because the statute of limitations was beginning to run out on some of the other defendants.

Nixon was totally relaxed and occasionally had his feet up on the desk as he questioned us. He listened to Buzhardt and me debate for perhaps forty-five minutes and then said, "I guess you have to indict him." Haig looked as if he would fall out of his chair at this, because Haig's understanding was that he was to dissuade, or at least delay us from going forward with the investigation. Nevertheless, Nixon reached the only possible conclusion on the facts as they stood.

Looking back, I'm not convinced Nixon ever really wanted to delay indictment proceedings against Agnew. He surely recognized from the outset that Agnew was fatally damaged, so it's hard to see what he accomplished by holding court to decide the issue. Perhaps there was a sense of loyalty to Agnew, the same feeling that got him into increased trouble later on when he tried to cover for his staff. But Nixon was aware, particularly from the Alger Hiss case, in which Nixon uncovered a spy ring operating at the direction of the Soviet Union, that it was the cover-up that more frequently brought down a defendant than the crime he was trying to conceal. (Even though the statue of limitations on charges of espionage had expired, Hiss was ultimately convicted of perjury.)

Historian Fred Emery thinks Nixon regarded Agnew as his "impeachment insurance," but by this point I think Nixon realized that impeachment proceedings against him might be forthcoming.[11] He needed time to nominate and confirm a new vice president before both he and Agnew were gone, lest the White House fall into the hands of the Democratic party, invalidating the votes of 47 million Americans.

Moreover, Nixon was extremely calm throughout the entire meeting—to the point that I began to ask myself whether staging a debate was Nixon's way of judging people. Or perhaps he was taking the opportunity as a sort of dry run to try and gauge how the Department of Justice would respond to his own predicament.

Nixon expressed a rather wistful regret: "Spiro has done everything I have asked him to." Then he turned to Richardson, adding, "If you're going to start cleaning up politicians take a look at . . ." and then he began to list various areas of the country in which corruption was ripe. I was surprised once more at his intimate knowledge of domestic politics, including its seamy side, as well as world issues.

They agreed that the case against Agnew would have to be argued by somebody whom they trusted not to make a carnival of the case or to make mistakes that Agnew's attorneys would embellish.

At the end of our discussion of the Agnew matter, Nixon turned to me and remarked, "Once these impeachment matters get started they go very fast, don't they? Once the process starts?" Unsure if he was referring to Agnew's fate or his own, I responded that I had only one example of a presidential impeachment to go by, but that it had taken the House and the Senate a month or two to impeach and try Andrew Johnson in 1868. It was clear that Nixon and Haig were thinking about impeachment quite seriously.

When we got back in the attorney general's limousine to return to the office, Elliot said I had just seen Nixon at his best, and mentioned he was surprised that Nixon had wanted me to be his chief defense attorney, since I was a professor. I told him that when I was in private practice I had put some complicated cases together; he expressed surprise and said nobody had told him that. He likened it to his own case, in which people overlooked the fact that he was a politician.

Once the White House made it clear to Agnew that the Department of Justice would be going forward with an indictment, Agnew became more amenable to resigning as part of a plea bargain. Press leaks of a potential agreement infuriated Agnew and led him to request, in a letter to the head of the House Judiciary Committee on September 25, that the House take up investigations related to the vice president. Agnew argued that the Justice Department was trying to usurp the function of the House. The only proper constitutional procedure, he argued, was for the House to investigate and hold impeachment hearings, and that the Justice Department ought not to interfere by going forward with the indictment.

We at the Justice Department responded with our own letter to the head of the House Judiciary Committee saying that we could not very well delay indictment, because the statute of limitations on various events was getting close to running out, but that as a matter of comity we would indict, and then pause to give the House a chance to start impeachment hearings if they wished. Speaker Albert rejected the request the following day, suggesting it related to matters before the federal courts and should be dealt with there.

On September 27, the grand jury began hearing evidence against Agnew. The following day Agnew's attorneys filed a motion in the United States District Court for the District of Maryland to prohibit the grand jury from hearing evidence against him on the grounds of vice presidential immunity. The vice president, they argued, could not be indicted and tried before he had been impeached and removed from office by conviction of that impeachment. They also filed a motion attempting to close down the grand jury on the grounds of prejudice stemming from press leaks they asserted were coming from the Department of Justice.

Lawyers from the Department of Justice met with Agnew's defense team before Judge Walter E. Hoffman on September 28, the day Agnew filed these two motions. In response to the second motion, the judge granted Agnew's attorney the subpoena power to try to determine the source of the leaks. In response, President Nixon held a press conference in which he backed the work of Henry Petersen, reasserting his full faith in Petersen's abilities and the investigation.

Back at the office the phone rang, and I knew at once what it meant. Elliot came on and said that he and the president agreed that I should argue the case against Agnew. Time was short. Briefs in response to both motions were due the following Saturday, just one week away.

The brief opposing the motion to close the grand jury posed no problems. The Justice Department frequently responded to such claims and routinely defeated them. We noted that we had no evidence to indicate the Department had anything to do with the leaks, and at the time I thought it was far more likely that Agnew's people were doing the leaking. (I have since learned that Nixon told Al Haig he suspected that "an important member of Richardson's staff" was the source.)[12] In any event, it isn't very hard for the press to get grand jurors to talk without any assistance from the attorneys on either side. But that was not grounds for stopping the grand jury; it was grounds for enjoining all the attorneys from talking.

The brief arguing that Agnew's position as vice president conferred no immunity from indictment proved much more difficult to write—particularly within our time restraints—as there was no authoritative law on the topic, and we had to create the law out of policy and the structure of the government. Fortunately, Keith Jones, an assistant of mine, had been reviewing a book by Raoul Berger on impeaching the president.[13] Although the then recently published book had created much excitement in the liberal press, it failed to deal immediately with any of the legal issues posed by the Agnew case. Jones knew Agnew's arguments were entirely derived from the president's immunity from indictment, suggesting the same immunity must be extended to the vice president.

This was, of course, a particularly delicate matter, as we had a president in danger of impeachment at the same time. So, while we had little trouble proving that Agnew did not have an office important enough to necessitate the presidential requirement of impeachment and conviction preceding indictment and trial, we had to take extra care to reaffirm that requirement for the president.

If a president could be indicted and forced to stand trial before being impeached and convicted, he would not officially be incapacitated to the point where the Twenty-fifth Amendment would apply, but he nevertheless would be effectively removed from heading the executive branch, impermissibly undermining its capacity to perform its constitutionally assigned functions.

The vice president, on the other hand, has very little relevance to governance as a matter of structure and practicality.

He becomes relevant only in the event that the president is removed from office, dies, resigns, or becomes incapacitated. Therefore, there is no compelling reason to require that the vice president complete the impeachment process before being indicted.

As it so happened, the Office of Legal Counsel also prepared a corresponding memorandum on the question of whether all federal civil officers are immune from indictment while in office. While they reached the same conclusion as the solicitor general's office, they did so in a diffuse and confused manner. At one point, the memo suggested the president could, in theory, with the aid of modern technology, run the executive branch from his jail cell, but perhaps such an arrangement "might be beneath the dignity of the office." Even suggesting that the president could run the free world from behind bars seemed so preposterous that, after reading an early draft of the memo, I insisted they take it out. Oddly enough, many people thought that the OLC memo was intended to assist Nixon in some way, or to head off any possibility of his indictment at any point. The memorandum was really so badly done, and so inconclusive, I was ashamed to think anybody might consider it the product of a conspiracy. If I was going to be suspected of such chicanery, I did not want the plot to suggest that I would rely upon such twaddle.

Edmund Kitch, a then–special counsel for the office of solicitor general (now a professor at University of Virginia Law School), provided counsel at this stage and throughout the Agnew affair as well. Over five hectic days, Kitch, Jones, and I put together the brief from scratch—a process that under normal circumstances would have taken a month or more—barely hitting the Saturday night deadline.

Through all of it, I had another case on my mind. In two days I was scheduled to make my first argument ever in the Supreme Court—as solicitor general, no less—so I returned to the office Sunday morning to read the key cases and briefs again as if cramming for an exam. I don't advise heading into the Supreme Court—or any court, for that matter—with one day's preparation, but I had no other choice.

One advantage of this hectic schedule was that I did not have time to become nervous about my argument. I got up Monday morning and put on the traditional dress for a government attorney arguing before the Supreme Court: gray-striped trousers, a cutaway coat (often called a morning coat), and a black tie. I referred to this costume as a "suit of lights," a reference to the costume worn by a matador. A black vest is also required, as I had learned the previous year when Andrew Frey, then-assistant to the solicitor general, showed up wearing the light gray vest of fellow Assistant Harry Sachse (which, for the record, had been worn by Sachse before the Supreme Court without arousing complaint) and Chief Justice Burger called our office to complain that "the attorney looked as if he were getting married."

On the Monday morning of October 10, while I was surviving my first argument in front of the Supreme Court, Agnew's attorneys were frantically subpoenaing journalists for questions regarding the press leaks. But by the end of the day their tone had changed, and word came that Agnew's attorney was seeking to plea bargain. My Supreme Court arguments went smoothly enough, and I rushed back to the office still thinking I needed to prepare for oral arguments against Agnew in the Maryland federal district court. It was then I got the news of Agnew's imminent resignation, which was offered and accepted that same day.

I am told that Richardson cited our brief as one of the reasons that Agnew chose to seek a plea bargain and resign. Richardson was fond of the brief; "muscular," he called it. In light of our brief, Richardson was prepared to make the evidence available to the House should it initiate impeachment proceedings, while the Department would go forward with a trial had there been an indictment.

Agnew resigned as vice president and pled no contest to a single charge of tax evasion, but faced no imprisonment. Though I was initially disappointed that Agnew got off so lightly, Richardson convinced me that it was the best course of action. He said with Nixon facing possible impeachment, it would be terrible for the country to have the president on trial in the Senate on charges of impeachment and the vice president simultaneously facing trial in a district court on criminal charges. The effect not only would damage domestic arrangements and politics but also would cause a drastic lowering of American prestige and influence internationally.

Throughout the Agnew mini-drama, I had an opportunity to judge the players at close range. Some have speculated that Nixon and Richardson did not want Agnew to inherit the White House, and conspired to squash any chance for his political survival once they learned of the bribery scheme. Others have suggested Nixon and Agnew worked in cahoots to make sure Richardson did not get the nod for the vice presidential nomination. I saw no evidence of either scenario. The players seemed to me to be defeated by their own characteristics. Spiro Agnew was an unlovable character whom nobody would put forward as a president, and Richardson simply did not possess the rhetorical skills needed to win votes.

To say as much about Richardson is not to discount the role he played as attorney general. It might be the solicitor general who wears the matador's suit of lights, but it's the attorney general who spends the most time in the big fights. The day after Agnew's resignation, Richardson, performing admirably, took to the podium in front of a group of reporters to defend the Department's handling of the investigation. After the press conference, he retreated with two aides to his favorite lunch spot, Jean-Pierre. Noticing a painting of a Spanish *corrida* hanging on the wall in the restaurant, Richardson empathized with the bullfighter. "The trouble with being a matador," he told his aides, "is that you have to face a new bull every Sunday."[14]

As Richardson would soon find out, sometimes the bull wins.

5

The Saturday Night Massacre

EVEN AS THE STRUGGLE with Agnew was going forward, Special Prosecutor Archibald Cox, himself a former solicitor general under President John F. Kennedy, had been investigating the possible involvement of Richard Nixon and any other White House personnel in the break-in at the Watergate complex. Up to this point I had been fortunate enough not to be involved in any way with the workings of the special prosecutor's office, and the rest of the Department had suffered no more than the expected minimal involvement occurring from two offices with so many overlapping responsibilities.

In some sense, the final showdown between Nixon and Cox was preordained. Simply by virtue of Cox's close relationship with the Kennedys, it's likely that a firm determination to be rid of him was set in Nixon's mind from the moment of his nomination.

Furthermore, as I mentioned earlier, Richardson wrote

the statement of jurisdiction for the special prosecutor practically overnight. As a result, it contained a paragraph so wide open it suggested that Cox and his staff could investigate anything that had to do with the White House, even though Richardson had intended to limit the charter to Watergate-related matters.

Cox understood the intended limit of the charter as well. To his credit, when it came to his attention that his staff had started to drift into issues such as whether Ehrlichman had been improperly involved in some apartment deal down south, Cox agreed that that was outside the scope of his duties and put an end to the wandering. Then again, the problem of an overeager staff was of his own making—Cox had staffed his office with volunteer lawyers and, as one might expect, those willing to perform for free the task of uncovering any and all impropriety surrounding Nixon and his administration were a hostile bunch.

Once Cox and his team were in place, there might not have been much Attorney General Richardson could have done to prevent an eventual showdown between Cox and the president. But by drafting an unnecessarily vague charter, choosing a known adversary to Nixon for the position of special prosecutor, and poorly managing Cox while he staffed a special prosecution team made up almost entirely of liberal Democrats, Richardson set in motion a series of events that would ultimately force his own resignation.

The irony was that the appointment of a special prosecutor probably delayed Nixon's exit from office. Until the arrival of Archibald Cox, the investigation into the Watergate break-in had been conducted by the U.S. Attorney's Office in Washington under the direction of Assistant U.S. Attorney Earl Silbert. Working assiduously, Silbert had much of the case already made by the time he handed Cox an eighty-seven-page memorandum summarizing his investigation's findings so far. It's a fair estimate that the material given to Cox composed 90 percent of the final case against Nixon. If anything, the time spent appointing a special prosecutor and getting him up to speed only delayed Nixon's otherwise sealed fate. The most notable difference between the two investigations is probably Silbert's limited focus on matters surrounding the Watergate break-in. For the most part, all the subsequent maneuvering and mudslinging from both sides was superfluous.

There is a certain irony in a special prosecutor's relations with the White House. Generally speaking, the special prosecutor system is rotten. True, there are cover-ups, and, at times, a special prosecutor could be crucial to uncovering them. But properly guarding against abuse would require the government to provide unlimited funds to the defense attorneys. Otherwise the special prosecutor, with access to unlimited funds, can spend and spend and spend until the defense is bankrupt and its only option is to plead guilty. I cannot see Congress writing an unlimited check to defense attorneys. When former Secretary of Labor Ray Donovan was finally acquitted of grand larceny and fraud in connection with a New York City subway construction project in 1987, he was told he could retrieve all of his belongings from the office in which they were being held and return to his job. Rejoined Donovan: "Which office do I go to to get my reputation back?"[1] In a similar way, those who appear in the crosshairs of a special prosecutor—guilty or not—tend to be left searching for their reputations for months and years to come. For the most part, the normal workings of the Department of Justice and of the press corps that cover a story should be enough to guarantee the exposure of wrongdoing without a special prosecutor.

Even if the case had stayed in the office of U.S. Attorney Silbert, Nixon's ultimate resignation was probably inevitable. Whoever lost in the district court would take the case to the court of appeals, and the loser there would surely appeal to the Supreme Court. It is impossible to imagine that the Supreme Court would uphold Nixon: the public would have been outraged by any ruling that left the ultimate question of Nixon's guilt up in the air. This was one of those cases Oliver Wendell Holmes spoke of as having "hydraulic pressure" behind it.[2]

My first contact with the special prosecutor's office came when Richardson called me in a few weeks after appointing Cox. The White House had expressed concern that the special prosecutor's staff was getting into national security matters. We had a meeting with Cox to discuss possible solutions, with little success.

The special prosecutor's staff continued to delve into matters with no relation to Watergate, as if their mission was to build a case of any sort against anybody in the administration. It was a delicate matter: when the executive office tried to define their jurisdiction, there were naturally protests charging that the special prosecutor's work was being hampered. The tension was inevitable. And as I mentioned earlier, Cox recognized that there had been transgressions by his staff and agreed that some limits had to be set. But, as I was to learn, even the special prosecutor's agreement could not prevent congressional demagogues from making the same charges.

In light of the expansive inquiries from the special prosecutor's office, Richardson assigned me the task of rewriting the special prosecutor's charter to make it clear that only Watergate-related matters were within Cox's jurisdiction. Whether Richardson thought he would actually be able to submit a new charter while Cox was still in place, I'm not sure.

At about the same time, Richardson asked me to deal with the special prosecutor's office concerning claims of executive privilege, particularly concerning the Oval Office recordings. "Executive privilege" is a poorly named doctrine that enables units of the government to preserve secrecy in important matters. It's poorly named because all units of government, not just the executive, claim that privilege. For example, if a litigant attempted to discover the contents of the judicial process to show that the Supreme Court's deliberations were somehow improper, he would be rebuffed by the Court's claim of immunity from disclosing such deliberations. Similarly, an attempt to subpoena the contents of a legislative deliberation would also be rejected. The term "executive privilege" makes the claim sound as if the executive branch alone claims the right of confidentiality and thereby arouses hostility to the claim.

Without some form of privilege, the deliberations of the branches of government and their agencies would be entirely artificial. People who know their thoughts and words may be made public will not speak with the freedom and candor they otherwise would. We are left to imagine politicians and bureaucrats striking poses appropriate to statues and uttering noble sentiments for public consumption. Someone with a sardonic frame of mind and the gift of turning a phrase would be fortunate to escape discharge or impeachment. A more accurate name for the claim of confidentiality might be "governmental privilege." (During the Ford administration, some of us in the Department of Justice began using this term in the hope that it would catch on, but it never did.)

Richardson sent me to negotiate an understanding on the proper role of executive privilege with Philip Lacovara, one of Cox's deputies from the special prosecutor's office. Richardson was quite worried about causing permanent damage to the privilege from overuse by the Department in litigation unrelated to Watergate. Lacovara, a former deputy in the solicitor general's office, was fully aware of the need for the privilege and sympathetic to our efforts to preserve it. He was also a member of the special prosecutor's staff, however, and aware that, in this instance, his office might have a sufficient need to overcome the privilege.

There was no formula that could resolve these contradictory interests. Lacovara went as far as he could by drafting document requests that were confined to the facts of the case the special prosecutor was pressing, but I could find no principle that limited these requests. In the end, we could find no common ground or formula to solve the dilemma of the privilege.

Other relationships between the White House and the special prosecutor continued to deteriorate. Cox had issued a subpoena for the White House tapes, as any competent prosecutor would be bound to do. Nixon, however, was inclined to see the demand as an instance of political attack. Neither side would budge.

Through all of it, the White House still had three major items on its plate: the Vietnam War (although the political drama had been reduced to a relative simmer in the weeks following the Cambodia bombing resolution); an escalating war in the Middle East, with the United States strategically aiding the Israeli forces as the Arabs received assistance from Moscow; and the process of finding a new vice president.

Nixon tackled the latter by orchestrating a highly public search for Agnew's replacement, culminating in a prime-time speech from the East Room in front of cabinet members, members of the diplomatic corps, and representatives from all the major media outlets. Always one to craft a moment, Nixon extolled the virtues of his selection while withholding his name until the last possible opportunity. Nixon's announcement of Gerald Ford, then the minority leader of the House of Representatives, as his selection for vice president received a grand response from the bipartisan audience.

As Nixon gathered, correctly in my opinion, Ford was

the only candidate who had both presidential stature and the ability to be approved by Congress. Alas, he was not Nixon's first choice. That distinction belongs to John Connally, a former Democratic governor of Texas (he was a passenger in the car with President Kennedy at the moment of his assassination and suffered wounds from the same "magic bullet" that struck Kennedy) and Treasury Secretary. Connally switched to the Republican Party in May 1973, and was being carefully groomed by Nixon to play a major role in the party for years to come. Ironically, the only thing that kept him from being the next vice president was being too suited for the job. Congressional Democrats, still sour from his shift of party, worried his appealing style of politics would lock them out of the White House for at least another eight years. When word spread that Nixon might be considering him for the vice presidential slot, Democrats vowed they would not approve him.[3]

Even though he didn't get his first choice, that jubilant evening in the East Room provided Nixon a brief reprieve from an otherwise disastrous few months. His confidence buoyed, Nixon decided that the escalating confrontation with Cox over the tapes could in fact be resolved outside the Supreme Court, one way or another.

The next morning, Haig called Richardson to the White House to discuss with him and Buzhardt how to resolve the tapes issue once and for all. In the same ego-inflating manner he used to try to convince me to be Nixon's chief defense counsel, Haig told Richardson he had the opportunity to help bring peace in the Middle East by dealing with Cox, who had single-handedly paved the way for war by weakening the U.S. president around the world.

After refusing the White House's first proposed solution for the president himself to prepare authenticated versions of the nine subpoenaed tapes, Richardson agreed to present Cox with a final proposal in which John Stennis, the senior senator from Mississippi, would scrutinize the tapes—withholding any sections with national security implications—and deliver the authenticated tapes to Cox. From a political perspective, the choice of Stennis was a brilliant move by the Nixon administration, for almost all members of Congress shared an opinion of him as a man of unquestionable integrity. Cox would have no choice, the White House reasoned, but to accept the compromise or resign (those in Richardson's office took to calling the plan "The Gospel According to St. John"). When Haig asked Stennis to do this favor for the president, and for his country, no less, Stennis—in poor health and still recovering from a mugging attack outside his home—indicated he would need some assistance to complete the task. The White House graciously offered Buzhardt's services.

The president stipulated to Richardson that when he presented this plan to Cox, Cox must understand that "this was it." According to Haig, when Richardson was asked what Cox would do when confronted with such an order, he replied that Cox would resign. Although there was some initial discussion about whether or not Richardson would fire

Cox should he refuse the order and still not resign, the issue was never decided definitively between Richardson and the White House.[4]

Had Richardson brought me to the initial meeting as he did during the Agnew affair, I'm confident there would have been more discussion of precisely what the next move would be if Cox should refuse the compromise. In many cases, the Nixon administration had thrived by implementing a policy of studied ambiguity. In this instance, the tactic would prove a fatal error. Richardson presented the proposal to Cox with a deadline for response of midnight Friday. To be sure, I report on the intricacies of these negotiations with relatively little insider information, as I was not privy to any of the immediate conversations.[5] The one sustained interaction I had with the main players from that week was on Wednesday evening, October 17. Claire and I attended an informal dinner party hosted by Richardson at his home, along with Ruckelshaus and several politicians. I remember Claire looking on with wonderment that she was at "a real Washington dinner party." Given what was going on that week, the innocuous conversation wasn't nearly as telling as the absence of a conversation that should have been going on.

For a while, it seemed as though the deal might go through. On Friday evening, the radio announced that the "Stennis compromise" had been worked out between Cox and the White House. I phoned Richardson to congratulate him at succeeding at such an enterprise: "God, I've just heard the news, Elliot! It's great!" With weariness in his voice, Richardson said that Cox was not, in fact, going along with the suggested compromise.

Still, I had no inkling that the dispute would in any way involve me. I went to work on Saturday and occupied myself with humdrum details of the office—including writing a letter to a third-grade class on "The Importance of Bill of Rights Day." Cox had announced a press conference to explain that he would not accept the Stennis compromise. When the announced time for Cox's press conference neared I walked down the hall to the press secretary's office to watch it on television. Cox gave an impressive performance, replete with the long-standing ritual in which the person giving the conference recites how he lay awake at night asking himself if he was doing the right thing or whether he was getting a bit above himself. Cox concluded that he was in fact doing the right thing, just as every other person giving such a conference does.

Cox maneuvered around the Stennis compromise by noting that, even though Stennis was a man of unquestionable integrity, "no one man" should carry the burden of preparing the tapes.[6] Noting Cox's careful attention to theatrics, one of my Yale colleagues later remarked, "I didn't know Archie could play Jimmy Stewart so well."

When Cox completed his presentation, Richardson's secretary appeared at the door to the press office and said that the attorney general wished to see me. I suspected he was seeking advice on what to do next, but I had no premonition of the role I would be asked to accept.

In Richardson's office I found Deputy Attorney General William Ruckelshaus and two or three of Richardson's young men who were part of his personal staff. Richardson outlined the state of play between the White House, Cox, and himself. He was being heavily pressed by Nixon to fire Cox, and had been back and forth from the White House several times. He was anxious to find a way around firing Cox while maintaining his relationships with the White House at the same time. After Cox's national television speech, that seemed increasingly impossible.

Then Richardson turned to Ruckelshaus and said, "I can't fire Cox. Can you, Bill?"

"No," Ruckelshaus said, "it would be wrong."

When Richardson turned to Ruckelshaus it suddenly occurred to me that by regulation I was third in line at the Department of Justice.

Richardson then turned to me and said, "Can you fire him, Bob?"

I was taken off guard. Richardson explained that he and Ruckelshaus were in different moral positions than I was. Richardson had given Cox a charter and had promised the Senate, as a condition of his confirmation, that he would fire Cox only on the stated basis of "extraordinary improprieties," as had Ruckelshaus.

"The gun is in your hand—pull the trigger!" he exclaimed.

"Give me a moment to think," I responded. I mulled my

options, which were few enough, and paced about the office while Richardson and Ruckelshaus continued a discussion and the young aides came in and out.

I am suspicious of anyone who describes himself as calm and logical in moments of crisis. When the question of whether to fire Cox came up, I was in a welter of contradictory impulses, unable to see clearly what the results would be of a firing or a refusal to fire. I recognized that the president had a clear legal authority to fire Cox and a good reason to do so. It seemed obvious to me that a lower-level executive officer could not publicly defy the president on national and, indeed, international television. The fact that Nixon was simultaneously attempting to rescue Israel from attacks by Egypt and Syria merely dramatized the point.

Furthermore, according to Department of Justice regulations, I was the last man in succession. Had I refused to fire Cox, it was extremely unlikely that any other political appointee would have been willing to take a temporary appointment as attorney general. The White House in turn would not want to risk offering the acting position to others in the Department, who might well turn it down with self-righteous rhetoric. Much more likely, a White House figure—perhaps Fred Buzhardt—would have been appointed as acting attorney general. The result, I feel confident in stating, would have been mass resignations at the upper levels of the Department of Justice. Regardless of his actual intentions, Buzhardt was known as a fierce political infighter, and there would have been reason to fear the dissolution of the special prosecutor's staff and a mass exodus in the Department of Justice.

On the other hand, the argument for not firing Cox was personal and none too credible. It was fear about the consequences for myself that made me hesitate. Once I got over those, the choice was clear.

Finally I said, "I can fire him, but then I will resign."

The look of relief on their faces quickly gave way to one of confusion. Richardson asked me why I would resign.

"I don't want to appear to be an apparatchik," I replied.

They then urged that for the good of the department and its continuity that I not resign. They voiced my same concern over the question of who would be appointed acting attorney general, and we spent the next few minutes trying to play out the possible fates of the Watergate investigation should I resign, none of which was acceptable. But not resigning would limit my ability to deflect the anger and the apprehension the firing would cause. Ruckelshaus reassured me that he and Richardson would say publicly that they had urged me to stay. Richardson was called back to the White House, and I took the opportunity to go down the hall to my office to call my wife and say, "I think I have to fire Archibald Cox."

She, of course, had not a suspicion that anything was in the wind. After a long drawn-out "Uhhh," she suggested I call Alex Bickel, as I had done in so many other crucial moments. I did, but Bickel, it turned out, was playing tennis and I had to do without his counsel.

I went back to Richardson's office. He came in after a lengthy session at the White House in which Haig and

Nixon had tried to persuade him to fire Cox. Instead, Richardson had tendered his resignation.

As Elliot came in, word came from Ruckelshaus's office that Haig wanted to speak to him. Knowing what was next, Ruckelshaus also refused to fire Cox and offered his resignation as well. (Ultimately, Nixon would not accept that Ruckelshaus was under the same obligations to Cox and the Senate as Richardson, and refused his resignation, choosing to fire him instead.) After a short time, Ruckelshaus returned and said, "Get ready for a phone call, Bob."

The call came through from Haig, who asked me to come to the White House. I think they knew that I was their last chance to get the discharge accomplished by a Department of Justice official, so they wanted to get me into the White House where it would be harder to escape. They sent a car over, and I went down and met it at the Department's Ninth Street entrance. Leonard Garment was in the passenger seat next to the driver, and Fred Buzhardt was in the rear. I began to laugh because it was so obvious that I was not to escape. I think I said something about being "taken for a ride." Nobody laughed.

When I got to Haig's office, he immediately began bloviating about the Middle East situation, and how the international strength of the president was in mortal peril.

I interrupted Haig to say that I had already decided I would fire Cox. "The only question is whether I resign after I do it." Charles Alan Wright was also in the room, and offered to draft a discharge letter. "Keep it terse, Charlie," I advised. The letter is reproduced here:

October 20, 1973

Dear Mr. Cox:

As provided by Title 28, Section 508(b) of the United States Code and Title 28, Section 0.132(a) of the Code of Federal Regulations, I have today assumed the duties of Acting Attorney General.

In that capacity I am, as instructed by the President, discharging you, effective at once, from your position as Special Prosecutor, Watergate Special Prosecution Force.

Very Truly Yours,
ROBERT H. BORK
Acting Attorney General

Immediately after the discharge letter was given to a messenger for delivery to Cox, I was taken in to see Nixon. My recollection is that the Oval Office was dim and shadowy, but that may be more a reflection of Nixon's and my mood than the room's physical condition. Nixon was distraught. He had not anticipated that Richardson would refuse to fire Cox and resign, nor that Ruckelshaus would subsequently do the same. He had blundered into what the press would deem the "Saturday Night Massacre" rather than planned it, but I suppose "Saturday Night Involuntary Manslaughter" didn't have the same ring.

In my conversation with him, Nixon made three remarks that took me by surprise. The first was the question Nixon asked me upon entering the Oval Office: "Do you want to be attorney general?"

"That wouldn't be appropriate," I responded.

I am certain Nixon was not offering me the job but rather was assessing the kind of man he had to deal with. I said it wouldn't be appropriate because I had decided from the first moment I realized I was going to be asked to fire Cox that if I carried out the discharge I could not profit personally, or even appear to profit, in any way. (My opinion in this regard remained steadfast—subsequently, as acting attorney general, I stayed in my regular office rather than moving into the more spacious quarters of the attorney general, and continued to use my solicitor general stationery with "Acting Attorney General" squeezed into the header. I also refused to use the car service allocated to the attorney general, much to the distress of his driver. One evening when I passed him in the parking lot, he jokingly complained that the tires on the car were deteriorating from lack of use. I continued to drive my ancient Volvo station wagon to the office, even though it was nearing the end of its life. It was a four-cylinder car, and two of those cylinders had stopped working. Not too long after that Saturday night, I discovered I had to take several runs to get the car up the ramp out of the Department's garage. When asked by a reporter why I refused the limo, I replied, "I don't enjoy playing Queen for a day.")

After emphasizing that all he wanted was "a prosecution, not a persecution"—which he clearly felt had been the tactic of the special prosecutor—Nixon then asked me who would be in charge of the Watergate investigation now that Cox was gone. I said the Criminal Division headed by Henry Petersen would take over.

That's when Nixon made a second surprising comment: "I'm not sure Henry Petersen is up for the task." I found the comment puzzling, as Nixon had vouched for Petersen's integrity and competence throughout the Agnew matter, when many thought Petersen was the source of the leaks to the press. I think Nixon mistook the deference Petersen thought he owed the president for vulnerability, but that is not my view at all.

And then, for the first and only time, Nixon said to me, "You're next when a vacancy occurs on the Supreme Court." I don't know whether Nixon actually, but mistakenly, thought that he still had the power to get me confirmed after the Massacre, or whether he was holding out the prospect in order to seal my continued loyalty. Whichever it was, I did not think it a promise that could be kept even if it were genuine. I hadn't the courage to tell him that I didn't think he could get anyone confirmed to the Supreme Court, and particularly not the person who fired Cox.

As soon as I left the Oval Office, I had the White House operators trying to reach Henry Petersen. He was, per his usual weekend custom, out with his wife on their boat in the Chesapeake Bay. I don't know how, but they got him ashore and to a phone on the end of the pier. I cut right to the chase: "Henry, I just had to fire Archibald Cox."

"Jesus Christ," Henry gasped.

"And Elliot has resigned."

He said something equivalent to his first response.

"And Bill Ruckelshaus has resigned."

His swearing increased in creativity. Quite understandably, he was flabbergasted. He had no idea any of this was going forward, and was therefore caught completely off-guard by the whole incident. I told him that I needed to see him as soon as possible, tomorrow morning at the latest. We arranged to get together on Sunday at the Department.

On my way out of the White House, I remarked to Haig that the news of Cox's firing and Richardson's and Ruckelshaus's resignations would come as a shock to the personnel of the Department. Haig asked me whether I would like him to come along to explain it to the Department. I declined, saying I would prefer to inform the staff myself. I saw a glimpse of approval in Haig's eyes because, had I asked for his assistance, it would have been a sign of weakness and inability to cope with Department personnel.

Returning to the Justice Department, I went directly to see Elliot Richardson. The solicitor general has a private elevator at the southeast corner of the Department of Justice Building, and the attorney general has a private elevator a block away on the southwest corner. In between, on the fifth floor, there was a gaggle of reporters seeking information as to the state of play with Cox. It would have been impossible for me, already identified as the man who fired Cox, to get down that corridor through shouted questions and camera lights that would block the way. So I took my elevator down to a lower floor, walked the length of the building through darkened offices in the Antitrust Division, and took the attorney general's elevator up to Richardson's office.

Together, we sat in his office and reviewed our options. He said the one thing he regretted was that he had perhaps not made it sufficiently clear to the president that he did not consider Cox's refusal to accept the Stennis compromise as such an offense of "extraordinary impropriety," though Cox's flamboyant rejection of the president's offer on national television might be construed as cause. In either case, the matter was far from clear.

It was an oddly wistful talk we had. Neither of us expected to have much future in government. I said that I had never enjoyed working with anyone so much as I had with him, and he said he felt the same way about me. We parted to our separate anticipated oblivions—Richardson to his limousine and me to my Volvo.

That evening, my wife and I threw a small dinner party for Ralph and Kate Winter because it was their anniversary. Ralph, who had been a colleague at Yale and was still a professor in the law school (and remains a dear friend), happened to be staying with us during this whole affair, and remembers much of that evening. In particular, he remembers overhearing a conversation I had with William Baroody, Sr., then president of the American Enterprise Institute for Public Policy Research, a Washington-based think tank. Baroody repeatedly urged me to give an order in my new position as acting attorney general that the special prosecutor's office was not to pursue any more tapes, or else I should fire the entire staff. According to Winter's recollection, I responded that I would be guided by what the Criminal Division said they needed for their investigations. Given Baroody's relationship with Nixon at the time, I suspect my response made its way back to the White House.

Much to my surprise, Jewel Lafontant, a woman whom Nixon had appointed deputy solicitor general at the same time I was nominated as solicitor general, called to congratulate me on my new gig as attorney general. Apparently she failed to understand the nature of the day's events. "Catastrophes," I responded, "don't call for congratulations."

That night, in the confusion that reigned, some of the special prosecutor's staff grew hysterical. Henry Ruth, Cox's chief deputy, was seen agonizing on camera that the situation was just like *Seven Days in May*, a novel and movie about a conspiracy among generals and top politicians to remove the president. This was not entirely an analogous situation, since the plotters in *Seven Days in May* were planning to remove the president, while Ruth was suggesting that the president was plotting to remove governmental powers from the top levels of the executive branch, including the Joint Chiefs of Staff. Phil Lacovara was calmer. He called me at home to ask whether I had received orders with respect to the rest of the staff. I told him I had not.

With that, the day of the Saturday Night Massacre came to an end. I went to bed restless with a laundry list of tasks awaiting me in the morning. I knew I could not resign, but still wished circumstances had allowed me to make the Massacre a murder-suicide.

Acting Attorney General Robert H. Bork
testifies before the Senate Judiciary Committee in
Washington, D.C., on Wednesday, November 14, 1973.

6

After the Massacre

I DROVE INTO WORK Sunday morning and had barely settled into my desk when Sol Lindenbaum appeared at my door. Sol was sort of the institutional memory of the Justice Department, a career employee who handled a lot of administrative details. He came in with a shamefaced grin and said, "I have something for you to sign as your first official act in your new position." As he set the papers on my desk with the same impish smile plastered on his face, I could tell he was waiting for me to take a look. I did, and instantly realized why he was waiting for my reaction. In an ironic stroke of cosmic proportions, the lease renewal forms for the Teapot Dome Oil Field had just arrived and required the signature of the attorney general.

Back during the Harding administration, Interior Secretary Albert Fall accepted bribes from private oil companies in exchange for leasing the Teapot Dome Oil Field in Natrona County, Wyoming, to the companies at absurdly low rates with no competitive bidding. For the next fifty years, "Teapot Dome" survived in the political lexicon as shorthand for political corruption—that is, until Watergate and the -gate suffix took its place. That William Safire didn't have the opportunity to spend a generation popularizing terms like Billydome, Contradome, Nannydome, and Climatedome is a tragedy all its own. Even in my exhausted, distressed state, I couldn't help but laugh. It seemed a fitting cap on the whole matter.

Monday morning—Veterans Day—my wife was too tired to make breakfast, so I went down to a local diner where I ate at the counter without anyone noticing me, or so I thought. When I got up to leave, I turned around to see a crowd flat against the window staring at me.

Since the offices had been closed for the holiday the day before, Tuesday was the first opportunity I had to sit down with Petersen and Cox's deputies Lacovara and Ruth to discuss how to keep order in the Department and maintain continuity in the Watergate investigation. Unsurprisingly, they tended to be more pessimistic about the state of things than were Petersen and I. Lacovara was sure the White House would not let the Justice Department complete the investigation. I responded that I intended to preserve the integrity of the investigation, and the only thing we could do was press forward and be fired if that was the way it turned out. We agreed that it was important for us not only to continue the investigation but also to do so in the most public way possible, so as to reassure the public that order was being maintained. At one point, I said I hoped that the special prosecutor's office had some good cases to work from, otherwise it might appear that we had not pressed hard enough. Lacovara said they did have a few such cases, and mentioned a senior Department official who was vulnerable to a charge of perjury. For reasons I did not and still do not fully understand, Henry Petersen then exploded and denounced Lacovara. I hurriedly tried to calm matters down; the last thing we needed was the resignation of Cox's deputies.

My recollection is that I told Lacovara and Ruth they could continue to subpoena tapes if it seemed called for. There is some dispute about this, but none about the fact that in a later meeting with the staff of the special prosecution force, I explicitly stated that they could subpoena whatever they needed for their investigation. I began by telling the staff I would not be discussing my decision to fire Cox, but would otherwise answer any questions. One staffer asked if they could still subpoena for necessary materials.

"I'll back you up," I told them. "Go to court for any tapes and documents you need, and resign if the White House gives you any trouble."

The decision earned me the enmity of both the White House and the special prosecution staff: The White House was sore because they didn't think I should make that concession, and a few members of the special prosecution staff felt slighted because, even though I approved the seeking of subpoenas, I still "had to be asked."

Later that day, I called a meeting of the senior staff of the entire Department of Justice—the heads of the departments, divisions, the FBI, the Bureau of Prisons, and so forth. They were naturally curious and uneasy about the developments of the past weekend. I explained that the only change was the departure of Cox and that the investigation would continue as before with the same people in charge, although they would now be listed as members of the Criminal Division rather than as members of a special prosecutor's organization. The staff seemed to find the explanation satisfactory, and I received no major complaints.

Most of the members of Richardson's and Ruckelshaus's staffs, as well as a few others from around the Department, resigned on what they claimed were moral grounds. None, of course, had made the same pledge to the Senate as did Richardson and Ruckelshaus. And a remarkable number of them resigned under circumstances that fit in with their career ambitions. One very junior lawyer accompanied his resignation with a letter expressing high moral sentiments of outrage over the firing of Cox and my continued presence. A few days later I heard that the same attorney had applied for a job in a different division of the Department and gotten it, so I suspect his outrage might have been more a matter of professional convenience. Cooler heads realized that if I had resigned, the Department would have been left leaderless and probably unable to find an acting attorney general within its ranks.

Work resumed its course in what, at the time, passed as normal. The legal processes were in place, the Watergate investigation continued, and the government continued to function. As one Department lawyer put it, "Yes, the mail is still delivered in the midst of the holocaust." What wasn't normal was the handling of the Department's work. The staffs of Richardson and Ruckelshaus, while not formally on any organization chart, had played important roles in keeping the attorney general and the deputy informed of developments within the Department and served as originators and critics of ideas. Now there was no one between the various agencies of government and me, including the heads of the Department's divisions. Paperwork came directly to me without the vetting the missing staffs had provided. I sat on a couch in my office and received emissaries from all parts of the government.

Throughout the turmoil, I relied upon the experience and instincts of Henry Petersen. As men will when they face a crisis together, Henry and I became close friends. Our sense of danger was heightened by the fact that nobody knew what the president might do. We spent long hours in my office, where we tried to anticipate events and our best reaction to them while Henry paced back and forth. Vast quantities of coffee were drunk by both of us. At one point, a senior White House official warned me that Nixon was fighting to retain the presidency and might take desperate actions of which I might not approve. Although he never did, the danger of what he might do hung over all our deliberations.

It is difficult to convey to today's readers the atmosphere of those days. The very air in the White House seemed rigid with anticipations of disaster. When a meeting ended and I left the building, it was like stepping from winter into springtime. My office was on the fifth floor of the Department of Justice, and I once, half-joking, gave orders that it be moved to the first floor so I would not seriously damage myself if I jumped in despair. It was then that I developed a deep admiration for Al Haig. He did a magnificent job of maintaining his balance while under pressure from Nixon in one direction and the Washington press corps and elites from the other. I decided he would make an excellent president, a conviction that remained with me until his heart operation, which seemed to cause a slight but important shift in his personality.

Recognizing the truth in the warnings about the president's possible desperate actions, I was determined not to be drawn into them and to preserve the distinction between what I owed the office of the presidency and what I did not owe to Richard Nixon as a man or a politician. Within the first few days, I sat down and wrote a statement of resignation, which I carried from then on in the breast pocket of my jacket to be used whenever the situation became perilous. I told Henry Petersen about the statement and without reading it he said, "Bob, if you think you have to resign, resign for me at the same time. Don't bother to check, just resign for both of us." Since it was addressed to unknown circumstances the letter was necessarily generic rather than specific, but I never had to use it.

Henry continued to be a close friend long after those daunting October days. During the early months of the Ford presidency, Henry's retirement date came due, and the Department threw a banquet in his honor at a local military base. I was the first speaker, and gave the one and only stem-winding speech of my career. It brought the crowd of several hundred to their feet; Henry and I clasped hands and held them high in the air while the cheering went on. A trifle taken aback by the enthusiasm and emotion on display, I turned and said to Henry, "Of course, there's always the other side."

Henry responded in kind, "There always is, Bob. There always is."

While there was little outrage within the Department of Justice, that was far from true outside the Department. The media crackled with outrage, and the general public for the most part seemed to agree. Mail poured in to my home and the telephone did not stop ringing until we couldn't take it, making my wife the only real estate agent in northern Virginia with an unlisted number.

Two things struck me about the firestorm that raged around us. The first was the poverty of moral rhetoric, and the second was the utter lack of careful thought on the part of even highly intelligent people. The poverty of rhetoric was illustrated by the constant equation of the dollar value of Yale degrees. The poor telephone operators at the Department fielded dozens of calls from Yale graduates upset that I had "lowered the market value of their Yale Law degree." That was preposterous on the face of it; nobody connected my actions with the value of having graduated from Yale. But even worse was the inability of so many Yale Law graduates to phrase their moral outrage in anything but monetary terms.

And then there was the inability of the press and public

alike to assess even the possible appropriateness and legality of Nixon's handling of Cox. A great many people praised the courage of Cox, Richardson, and Ruckelshaus, and I am willing to concede that a reasonable case can be made for each of them having behaved properly—either in refusing to obey a presidential order or in resigning—given the positions in which they found themselves (though not necessarily in the fashion Cox chose to parade his refusal). But a great many people seemed eager to turn them into American heroes. Cox went to Columbia to meet with a group of student radicals, and after entering through a window to address a raucous group of undergraduates, proclaimed them "the most enlightened and reasonable generation of students ever."

Richardson's refusal to fire Cox launched him on a wave of popularity that, it seemed for the moment, might carry him to the presidency. But Elliot's speeches cut off any such possibility. For a man of intelligence and ambition, Elliot Richardson had the worst speaking style imaginable. The columnist George Will once wrote that Elliot's speeches should be taped and then played to quell prison riots. Shortly after his resignation, he spoke in Pittsburgh, entering the hall to a standing ovation. After his delivery he left to a smattering of polite applause. It always puzzled me that he never sought advice on public speaking.

The confusion in the public mind was illustrated by one lawyer who told me quite confidently that I should have refused to fire Cox, as it would have brought Nixon down sooner. I responded that driving a president from office was not in my job description. If a constitutionally inferior officer of the executive branch could topple the president of the United States, then the country would begin to resemble a banana republic. There are constitutionally prescribed methods for ousting an unwanted president: impeachment by the House and conviction on the article of impeachment by the Senate. Anything else is civil disobedience, which, when the media is unanimous in attacking the president, resembles nothing so much as mob rule.

Had I held a press conference immediately after firing Cox to explain all of this—that the president had ordered "a prosecution, not a persecution" and had not asked me to do anything other than fire Cox—perhaps some of the flames might have gone. But, being new to the ways of Washington, the thought of a preemptive press conference never crossed my mind. Nor did anyone in the White House suggest such a conference. I doubt, however, that a statement to the press, no matter how reasonable and modulated, would have diminished their full-throated cries about a constitutional crisis that never was.

I do, however, think Nixon made a fundamental political miscalculation in dealing with Cox. He did not have the support of the universities and the intellectual class generally that John F. Kennedy or even Lyndon Johnson could muster. Nixon was, as Wills suggested, playing the tough guy because he had to. He should have replaced his regular mode of studied ambiguity with clear and concise explanations to the public.

Throughout the matter, I was surprised and disappointed at the failure of so many lawyers to act like lawyers. Prone to complimenting each other as "specialists in process," many lawyers demonstrated during the week after the Massacre, and throughout the Watergate affair, how easy it is to let process take a backseat to preferred political results. For those who found their liberal identity before embarking on a career as lawyers, they regarded Nixon as *ipso facto* outside the law. So long as lawyers persisted in castigating Nixon, so long would they forfeit the respect due a learned profession.

7

Restoring Justice

I HAD NOT BEEN LONG in my temporary position of acting attorney general when it became obvious that we would need to find a new special prosecutor to complete the Watergate investigation. Strictly speaking, we didn't need a special prosecutor. I'm confident the individuals we had in the office possessed the demeanor and intelligence necessary to see the Watergate investigation through to its inevitable conclusion. But with the outcry over Cox's firing reaching a fever pitch, the need for a new special prosecutor became a necessity, if only to calm everyone down.

In our independent searches for a new special prosecutor, the White House and the Justice Department hit on Leon Jaworski's name at about the same time. There was really no other candidate so well fitted for the job. Jaworski was a former president of the American Bar Association, and one of the first prosecutors at the war crimes trials before they moved to Nuremberg. We went through the list of other bar association presidents, but that was a fruitless enterprise. Jaworski was the one candidate suitable for the position. The others were too old for the job, lacked trial experience, or were otherwise disqualified.

Haig and I were equally enthusiastic about Jaworski, but perhaps for different reasons. Haig kept saying, "We have to get a real professional this time." Finding a real professional was easy enough. The difficulty was finding one that the bar and the press would accept as sufficiently independent and skillful enough to reassure the public that the new special counsel could be trusted. That required a sufficiently broad experience. Jaworski fit the bill.

After meeting with Haig, Jaworksi came to my office to interview with Petersen and me. He arrived with a sheath of résumés, which was quite unnecessary at this point. Petersen cast an eye over one of the résumés, and playfully turned to me to say, "Bob, he wasn't in the Corps!"—an inside reference to my known preference for Marine Corps veterans. I didn't say much by way of response, because I didn't want to do anything that might scare Jaworski away. We wanted him. Jaworski looked slightly bemused, but took the job anyway.

The appointment of Jaworski meant the creation of a new charter, a process in which Congress was decidedly interested. In what turned out to foreshadow events to come, the reestablishment of the special prosecutor charter provided an occasion for me to learn something of the reckless disregard for truth that was Senator Ted Kennedy's key to power.

In order to guarantee the independence of the special

prosecutor after Cox's firing, we tried adding to the new charter language to the effect that even with cause a special prosecutor could not be fired without the agreement of key individuals. When I was summoned before the Senate Judiciary Committee, Kennedy maintained that I had devised a means for firing the special prosecutor again. I called Jaworski, who understood the extra protection given by the clause in question and had no objection to it. But when I went before the Judiciary Committee again to explain that we had, if anything, strengthened the charter, Kennedy did everything in his power to paint the clause as a route to attack the independence of the special prosecutor. It was so obviously a false claim that even some members of the press folded their notebooks and left the hearing room. The upshot was a day of wasted time and nothing more. But I got a foretaste of Kennedy's willingness to say anything to gain a political advantage.

At this point, Nixon's unpredictability had reached a point where I began to worry I would be asked to do something that would force me to resign. Henry Petersen made up a list of all the political appointees in the Department who were left to run the Department, should worse come to worst. We extended the line of succession in the Justice Department five assistant attorneys general deep, just to be sure.

A few weeks into my stint as acting attorney general, my secretary, Mrs. Satterwhite, rang through to say that two gentlemen from the FBI were there to see me. Immediately all my free-floating anxieties coalesced. I had been operating without much staff and in a hurry. God knows what I had missed and the FBI had found. When they came in, I was relieved to learn that they were not there to clap me in irons, but relief soon gave way to distress as I learned what prompted their visit.

The FBI desired to appeal an adverse district court ruling about the Bureau's Counterintelligence Program (COINTELPRO), a program of intelligence gathering and disruption of various radical groups. As I recall, three of us met in my office: Clarence Kelley—who was the new head of the FBI—a longtime FBI executive, and myself. The executive was insistent that national security required continuation of the program. I said that, in my best judgment, we would lose the case and do so resoundingly. The man did not give up easily and pressed his points until Kelley, who had seemed undecided, now spoke for the first time. He said the program was wrongheaded. I tried to make clear to the FBI executive that a radical group could be planning violence or other criminal activity while also conducting fairly ordinary politics aboveboard. It was, I said, legitimate for the FBI to spy on and disrupt plans for violence or crime, but not on the conduct of regular political activity.

Of course, the distinction between national security and domestic wiretaps grew extremely blurry at times. For example, the Soviets summarized conversations or other information they received from domestic sources here and sent it by encrypted radio messages to Moscow. Our intelligence agencies and other intelligence agencies picked up the

Soviet messages and deciphered them. Since the Soviets were sending messages involving conversations with leading U.S. politicians, our intelligence gathering affected domestic as well as international matters.

While in the ordinary criminal case the government had time to obtain a warrant from a single judge, in national security matters sensitive classified information could not safely be submitted to judges scattered around the nation in order to obtain a warrant. In one case a federal district court judge read all the classified documents aloud in his courtroom, an absurdity that persuaded me to authorize searches and seizures without warrants.

A few years later, Congress created a special court, the Foreign Intelligence Surveillance Court, whose members are appointed by the Chief Justice from district court judges. I had serious doubts about the constitutionality of such a court, but the Foreign Intelligence Surveillance Act, which created this court, may be the least exacerbating of congressional reactions to Watergate. The War Powers Resolution, passed by Congress over the veto of Nixon in November 1973, expanded congressional control over the limits of presidential authority in the use of force abroad. Had the president asked for my advice, I would have suggested that instead of vetoing the Resolution, and thus giving it the dignity of a statute, Nixon should have returned the bill to Congress with a note saying he thanked them for their essay on his constitutional powers and, when he found time in his busy schedule, he would send them an essay of his own on his understanding of his constitutional powers. This would have treated the War Powers Resolution with the frivolous gesture it deserved.

Similarly misconceived were the 1974 amendments to the Federal Election Campaign Act, which, in seeking to purify the election process by taking money out of it, severely restricted campaign contributions. The result was to diminish political activity supposedly protected by the First Amendment. Eugene McCarthy's campaign, which drove Lyndon Johnson from office, could not have been conducted without very large campaign contributions. The result of the Act was that members of Congress spent more and more of their time begging for money and less and less in sober contemplation of their legislative duties. Attorney General Edward Levi and I regarded the statute as so blatant an attack upon First Amendment freedoms that I assigned the briefing and defense of the statute to a few senior deputies while Levi and I filed an *amicus curiae* brief questioning the Act's premises and assumptions. The *amicus* brief was written by Frank Easterbrook, then an assistant in the office of the solicitor general, and A. Raymond Randolph, then a deputy solicitor general. Both went on to distinguished careers in the law (as did so many of the young attorneys we had in the office at that time) and are now federal appellate judges. The Supreme Court saw fit to address the questions we raised with equivocation and compromise.

Watergate also prompted a move in Congress to make the special prosecutor a permanent part of the government, freed from any effective control by the attorney general or the president. We managed to fight off that obviously unconstitutional proposal throughout Gerald Ford's term as president, but Jimmy Carter, over the objection of Attorney General Griffin Bell, saw fit to honor his campaign promise to create a permanent special prosecutor. The difficulties with the statute are manifold, but the most obvious is its removal of the law enforcement function from the attorney general, despite the fact that the Constitution places it there. The excrescence persisted, to the delight of Democratic lawmakers, until it began to be used against Democratic presidents, at which point its evils became apparent to them.

•

In any case, with Jaworski in place and the continuity of the Watergate investigation intact, I was eager to see Nixon complete the process of confirming a new attorney general so I could return to my post as solicitor general. In the highly charged atmosphere of the time, the task would not be easy. Nixon solved the problem by choosing a safe senator, William Bart Saxbe of Mechanicsburg, Ohio. The press officer for the Department of Justice took care to help Saxbe smooth his rather rough-hewn mannerisms and add a patina of sophistication. That effort was set back a bit when Saxbe welcomed a reporter to his home. According to legend, Saxbe and his wife were giving the reporter the grand tour when they arrived at one of the spare bedrooms. Above the bed was a large painting of a nude. The trio stopped before it and the Saxbes, gesturing toward the painting and nodding knowingly, said in tandem, "Inspiration."

William Saxbe had a number of habits that might be

called colorful, including the grotesque habit of drooling tobacco spit from his bottom lip into a coffee tin. He didn't spit—he drooled. Drooled in his limo, and in his office; in private, and with company. A more gruesome sight I never saw. It got to the point where I took to breaking protocol in entering his office when there were several people going to meet with him. As solicitor general, I was traditionally supposed to be first to enter and take the seat closest to him. I took to waving in people ahead of me and taking a seat farther away so I didn't have to sit within eyeshot. Habits aside, a more vigorous attorney general I never saw. After he was confirmed in December, I was able to return to my duties as solicitor general.

Jaworski was pressing forward with preparations for the Supreme Court arguments over the subpoena of the White House tapes. I was called to the White House to find a small gathering in Haig's office consisting of James St. Clair, who was the recent addition to the president's defense team, and three or four other members of the White House staff. Haig said the president wanted me to argue the case defending his retention of the tapes in the Supreme Court. I said that if I did, my next argument would be before the grievance committee of the Illinois Bar Association explaining why I should not be disbarred, since I would have argued on both sides of the case.

I reminded Haig that the special prosecutor was a branch of the Department of Justice and that I was, nominally at least, his superior, making it impossible for me to go to court to take a position in opposition to the special prosecutor. Haig said I was relying upon a technicality.

"They hang people on technicalities!" I rejoined.

During a break in the action a few moments later, St. Clair whispered to me, "I think you're right."

I whispered back, "Tell him that," nodding toward Haig.

"Maybe I will . . . someday." That reply lowered my estimation of St. Clair, who was apparently more concerned with keeping the boss happy than providing candid legal counsel.

"Why don't you get Charles Alan Wright to argue your case for you?" I suggested to Haig.

He responded that Wright didn't have the constitution for the job. He meant it literally—word had spread that every time Wright got a call from the White House, he got physically ill to the point of vomiting. Nor was Haig thrilled with Wright's flamboyant statement to the district court in handing over the subpoenaed tapes, when he asserted, "*This* President obeys the law," leaving the question of which presidents didn't obey the law unanswered.

Both Wright and St. Clair signed the brief filed in the Supreme Court on the president's behalf. It was assumed, I think correctly, that the major part of the brief dealing with the Constitution was the work of Wright, who had a reputation as a constitutional scholar that the others lacked. A member of the prosecutor's staff characterized the brief as "random historical observations."

It became particularly apparent that St. Clair, and perhaps the entire defense team, did not understand that their only chance for a win was to make the argument that the Court had no jurisdiction to decide the case. Article III of the Constitution forbids federal courts from taking due jurisdiction where there is no case or controversy, and there was certainly an argument to be made that there was no such case for Nixon. That is, if Nixon was within his constitutional right to handle the dispute by giving the special prosecutor an order not to go to court for subpoenas (although such an order would be political suicide), then there was really no controversy for the Court to address. That it was politically impossible for him to do so does not affect the constitutional argument at all.

St. Clair did once make reference to this line of reasoning when arguing before the Supreme Court. Justice Potter Stewart replied that ordinarily the Court would not take on an intrabranch dispute, but here the prosecutor had a charter. In Stewart's view the existence of a charter seemed to give rise to a case or controversy that would not otherwise exist and therefore created an otherwise deficient jurisdictional base for the Court. The obvious rejoinder missed by St. Clair was that, if a charter was enough to plunge the Court into intrabranch disputes, the president or his surrogates could convert every intrabranch squabble into a justiciable dispute merely by issuing paper charters. That should have been enough to turn the Court away from the case, but of course it did not.

It is possible to have some sympathy for the Court's lawless assumption of jurisdiction. Every other means of getting the White House to produce the tapes had failed. It was

Jaworski's subpoena or nothing. Had the Court announced that it had no jurisdiction on a point that 99 percent of the population would not understand, the reaction would have been explosive. The episode is a useful reminder that all too often the Court cannot or will not stand in the way of an impassioned public.

After the decision against the president came down, Haig called me from the White House and said they were still discussing whether to obey the Court's order. "If you don't, it is instant impeachment," I said, which seemed to cast a new light on the dispute for Haig. I have no idea whether my opinion had any influence upon the outcome of the debate within the White House, but shortly afterward the president decided to release the tapes to Jaworski.

When the time came for Jaworski to go to court to report on the outcome of his subpoena, he called me on the telephone to warn me that Nixon's tapes were not complete. In particular, there was an unexplainable eighteen-minute gap in the tapes, which apparently could not be retrieved by any technology then available. The announcement of the gap marked the beginning of the final lap of the Nixon presidency, and it would unravel over the next year. Facing impeachment in the House and almost certain conviction in the Senate, Nixon announced his resignation, making Gerald Ford the new president of the United States. In the end, I think Ford's handling of the Nixon case was admirable. Had Ford pushed on with a criminal trial following Nixon's resignation, the result would have been catastrophic, both for our system of justice and for our politics.

Flanked by Acting Attorney General Robert H. Bork and Secretary of State Henry Kissinger, President Richard Nixon speaks during a meeting with the Cabinet Committee on International Drug Control and the Domestic Council Committee on Drug Abuse at the White House in Washington, D.C., on November 27, 1973.

EPILOGUE

I STAYED ON AS SOLICITOR GENERAL for the first few years of the Ford administration, leaving my post on January 20, 1977. Later that summer, I moved the family back to New Haven. Returning to Yale was not my only option. I was concerned that the firing of Cox would be used as a kill shot against me, but it turned out to be not much of a barrier anywhere. Several universities approached me to apply for open positions. I was asked if I wanted to interview for the presidency of Johns Hopkins University in Annapolis. The University of Michigan and the University of California, Los Angeles also approached me with offers. Turning those down was a simple matter of money and prestige; Yale had more of both. The most peculiar offer was for a chair in history at Princeton. The facts that I had no prior relationship with the university and very little formal training in history made the offer particularly strange.

Looking back, I think the source of the curious invitation can be traced back to Professor Arthur Link, a biographer of Woodrow Wilson, who heard me speak someplace and was impressed. I also think they were looking for a conservative. They had none on the faculty, and many alumni were in open revolt over the hiring of Peter Singer.

There were also a few offers outside of academia. I was offered a partnership at the international law firm of Rogers & Wells (now Clifford Chance). William Rogers was attorney general under Dwight Eisenhower while I was still at Yale, and was Nixon's secretary of state until Henry Kissinger maneuvered him out of his socks and took his job. Rogers was quite explicit when he called me up as to the seriousness of the offer, and mentioned they didn't have anyone famous—to which I questioned why they would want me.

I also entertained an offer to write part-time for *Fortune* magazine, and to spend the other half of my time in a post at the City University of New York. Ed Levi was really pushing me toward that option, warning me that going back to Yale would amount to little more than "following the conventional path." He was probably right. But I had a friend on the faculty at Yale who had moved heaven and earth to get me an offer back at my old post, and I still considered New Haven my home.

I don't regret my decision to return to Connecticut. Six years earlier, Claire had contracted cancer, and by the time I left the job as solicitor general she had grown quite weak. She also developed a close and trusting relationship with her tremendous team of doctors at the Yale–New Haven

Hospital. Being close to her doctors and without the stress of a new and unfamiliar environment was a top priority.

Claire died in December 1980 after a struggle of nine and one-half years, a fight fueled by her determination to see our children safely into adulthood. Though I knew it would be, her death was devastating to me. There was nothing left for me at Yale: my best friend, Alex Bickel, had himself died of cancer in 1974, and all my children were gone from home. New Haven had too many shadows.

I returned to Washington with the full intention of rejoining Kirkland & Ellis—the same firm I had left nineteen years earlier. In fact, I had already accepted a position there when I was approached by the Reagan administration about accepting a judgeship on the United States Court of Appeals for the District of Columbia Circuit. I said no to the first official who approached me, and no to the second official. I then received back-to-back phone calls from the very insistent Deputy Attorney General Edward Schmults and Attorney General William French Smith. "These guys must be serious," I thought to myself. After discussing the matter with my children, I decided to accept the offer.

One of the judges on the D.C. Circuit Court asked why I decided to leave practice for the bench. I told him that, having just lost two cases, I decided I was losing my fastball and had better take up umpiring. Another judge quipped, "I hope you didn't bring your curve ball."

On June 4, 1982, I spoke at a luncheon sponsored by the Ethics and Public Policy Center in Washington, D.C., and met the woman who would become my wife, Mary Ellen

Pohl. After two incidental meetings we had three dates, were engaged in July, and married in October at St. Matthew's Cathedral. The ceremony would have been sooner, but the church was not available.

I served six years on the D.C. Circuit Court with no indication that the Reagan administration was counting on me for the Supreme Court. Nixon clearly had me in mind for the Court. When Gerald Ford came into office, then–Attorney General Ed Levi said there were three of us he was considering for the Court. One of them was John Paul Stevens, who was in fact nominated by Ford in 1975. Another was Dallin Oaks, a Mormon, who was at that time president of Brigham Young University. Before that he taught at the University of Chicago, where we became good friends and spent many late nights together in the law library.

When President Reagan nominated me for the Supreme Court in 1987, I thought my confirmation was a sure thing. The Supreme Court had not overturned a single ruling of mine during my stint on the D.C. Circuit Court, and the Senate had confirmed Antonin Scalia 98–0 just a year earlier. It would be a wonderful job, and I figured the confirmation process would go smoothly enough.

I don't wish to rehash the entire Supreme Court nomination process in this space. On that debacle, I've spoken my piece. But among some of the more ludicrous questioning sessions (an exchange with then-Senator Biden, where he argued that an anticontraceptive law might lead to magistrates authorizing wiretaps to find out if couples were using contraceptives, ranks among the most memorable), I was asked about my time as solicitor general and my involvement in the Saturday Night Massacre. Although several senators from the Nixon era were still around who still considered my firing of Cox a disqualifying evil, the press spent relatively little time rehashing the Saturday Night Massacre or my time as solicitor general. The reason, I suspect, had as much to do with incompetence as anything. One reporter asked my son, "What's the solicitor general?"; another asked him to explain federalism.

Much of what I have recounted here I said during my hearings for the Supreme Court, alas, with more precision about the nuanced details, timelines, and exchanges. But now, with the opportunity to reflect on those fateful months in 1973 alongside the rest of my career, I am reminded of one moment near the very end of those Senate hearings that, while I did not realize it at the time, speaks to the whole of my experience in the Nixon administration and merits a few final thoughts.

"The law is not a place for the artist or the poet," Oliver Wendell Holmes, Jr., told a group of Harvard undergraduates. "The law is the calling of thinkers."[1] Holmes and his colleagues would presumably be aghast at what the profession of law has turned into. Now it is more accurate to say that the law is a profession of feelers who judge everything related to the courts from a political point of view.

There could be no better demonstration of the decline of law than the now farcical nature of Supreme Court confirmation hearings. During the confirmation hearings for Chief Justice John Roberts, one senator wanted to be reassured that Roberts would "be on the side of the little guy."[2] Another senator, who had "absolutely no doubt in [his] mind Judge Roberts is qualified to sit on the highest court of the land," nevertheless refused to vote for him on a personal calculation that Roberts "far more often used his formidable skills on behalf of the strong in opposition to the weak."[3] The same senator would later reaffirm, as president of the United States, that his nominees for the highest court in the land would possess the "quality of empathy, of understanding and identifying with people's hopes and struggles as an essential ingredient for arriving at just decisions and outcomes."[4]

These formulations of the "quality of empathy" as an "essential ingredient" and "big guy versus little guy" are useless in terms of jurisprudence; they also call upon a judge to violate his oath:

> I, (name) do solemnly swear (or affirm) that I will administer justice without respect to persons, and do equal right to the poor and to the rich, and that I will faithfully and impartially discharge and perform all the duties incumbent on me as ________ under the Constitution and laws of the United States. So help me God.

A fundamental misunderstanding of jurisprudence and the proper relationship between the law and those who swear to uphold it pervades Capitol Hill. It has for quite some time.

Which brings me back to my own experience in front of the Senate Judiciary Committee as a Supreme Court nominee. Near the end of the hearings, Senator Alan Simpson asked me one final question: "Why do you want to be an associate justice of the United States Supreme Court?"

It's an odd question; ordinarily you would take it for granted that any judge wants to be elevated to the Supreme Court. Being asked that question—in that setting—is meant to mark a shift in the pageant from the talent portion to the personal interview.

I am willing to concede that a more politically calculated account of the judicial duty would have been more appropriate to the tastes and capacities of the senators. It is still difficult to comprehend why my answer created such a stir:

> Senator, I guess the answer to that is that I have spent my life in the intellectual pursuits in the law. And since I've been a judge, I particularly like the courtroom. I like the courtroom as an advocate and I like the courtroom as a judge. And I enjoy the give-and-take and the intellectual effort involved. It is just a life and that's of course the Court that has the most interesting cases and issues and I think it would be an intellectual feast just to be there and to read the briefs and discuss things with counsel and discuss things with my colleagues. That's the first answer.

It's the bit about the job being an "intellectual feast" that sent the chattering classes rushing to their fainting couches. They could not grasp that a philosophy of jurisprudence enhances a judge's ability to navigate the thickets of the law.

The intellectual feast language, however, did not stand alone. It was accompanied with a second answer, ignored then and forgotten now, which not only should have been more acceptable to the senators but also captures a motivating force throughout my career, those hectic days in 1973 in particular:

> The second answer is, I would like to leave a reputation as a judge who understood constitutional governance and contributed his bit to maintaining it in the ways I have described before this committee. Our constitutional structure is the most important thing this nation has and I would like to help maintain it and to be remembered for that.[5]

To be sure, the solicitor general is an advocate, not a judge, with a different role and different responsibilities toward the maintenance of our constitutional structure. And yet, I still hope to be remembered as someone who did his part in that effort.

During the Saturday Night Massacre, I was called upon to step out of my role as solicitor general in order to fire Cox. It was a duty to justice—to keeping the government running—that convinced me to follow the president's order, and to remain long enough to hold together the Watergate investigation and the Justice Department as a whole. Without a soldier in the streets, we managed a transfer of power that would have shattered many nations.

And yet, without a preexisting love for the "intellectual feast" of law, I'm not sure I would have had the wherewithal to make the correct decision that October night. Whether in a role as judge or as advocate, my two answers to the Senate Judiciary Committee are flip sides of the same coin. A life in the law requires a sense of both inquiry and duty. Without inquiry, duty slips into idolatry; without duty, inquiry descends into navel-gazing.

What joys, then, has a life in the law provided? What has it taught? In moments of despair, I used to advise young people, most of whom seem headed for law school these days, not to go into the law. One former student reminded me that I advised his class to take up dermatology, another that cosmology would be preferable. I didn't really mean that, of course, and have since ceased saying as much. A life in the law can provide money—for some people, lots of money. More important, it provides excitement, humor, intellectual vigor, camaraderie with interesting people, and the satisfaction that comes from hard work done well.

The academic branch of the profession provides many of the same benefits (law school professors are surprisingly well paid) and, for the ambitious, the endless pleasures of intellectual striving to understand reality in ways the courts have not. For others, the academic life provides what someone called "the leisure of the theory class." There is a danger of middle-age burnout in both practice and teaching, but that is not inevitable and can happen in any line of work.

The life lessons learned are somewhat gloomier. The advance in the courts of one aspect of the law always seems to deteriorate some other aspect. Constitutional law is the most common victim, as it increasingly becomes little more than a cultural and political playground for judges and professors. They are playing with the most profound questions of culture, government, and social order. On the whole, their frivolity, and it can only be called that, has produced a glut of regrettable results.

There may be hope for the academy. The students of the late sixties and early seventies who went on to teach constitute a lost generation of constitutional scholarship, but recently some young professors have appeared who take the study of the Constitution quite seriously, as more than just a form of advocacy for desired social results. They may just conceivably make that body of law intellectually respectable again in the schools.

As for the courts, such an accomplishment will take a very long time, if it can be done at all. With each issue it takes out of the hands of the people in order to please the elites, the Supreme Court moves from being what my friend Alex Bickel called "the least dangerous branch of government" to a place where it can lay fair claim to being the most dangerous.

It bears endless repeating that we are now being ruled in some of our most crucial cultural and moral issues by judges who have acquired the power, but certainly not the authority, to take those decisions out of our hands. There is good reason to believe that this authoritarianism has become an inherent characteristic of most judges ever since the time they realized the full extent of their power and their relative invulnerability. In that capacity, they continue their attack on the basic structure of the law by filling the categories of law with politics. Originalism provides hope that the constitutional structure of our country will be maintained.

NOTES

Chapter 1: Getting the Job

1. Robert H. Bork, "Why I Am for Nixon," *The New Republic*, June 1, 1968.
2. Sanford J. Ungar, "The Undoing of the Justice Department: After the 'Saturday Night Massacre,'" *The Atlantic* (January 1974).
3. Federal Bureau of Investigation, Office of Planning and Evaluation, *FBI Watergate Investigation: OPE Analysis*, File Number 139-4089, July 5, 1974, 11.
4. Ungar, "The Undoing of the Justice Department."

Chapter 3: William O. Douglas's War

1. Stephen M. Millett, "The Air Force, the Courts, and the Controversial Bombing of Cambodia," *Air University Review* (July–August 1976), http://www.airpower.maxwell.af.mil/airchronicles/aureview/1976/jul-aug/millett.html.
2. See, e.g., *Mitchell v. United States*, 386 U.S. 972 (1967); *Mora v. McNamara*, 389 U.S. 934 (1967); *Massachusetts v. Laird*, 400 U.S. 886 (1970); *DaCoasta v. Laird*, 405 U.S. 979 (1972); *Mitchell v. Laird*, 488 F.2d 611 (D.C. Cir. 1973).

3. *Holtzman v. Schlesinger,* 484 F.2d 1307, 1308 (2d Cir. 1973).
4. *Holtzman v. Schlesinger,* 361 F. Supp. 553, 565 (E.D.N.Y. 1973), *rev'd,* 484 F.2d 1307 (2d Cir. 1973).
5. Millett, "The Air Force, the Courts, and the Controversial Bombing of Cambodia."
6. *Holtzman v. Schlesinger,* 414 U.S. 1304, 1315 (1973) (Marshall, J., in chambers).
7. *Holtzman v. Schlesinger,* 414 U.S. 1316, 1320 (1973) (Douglas, J., in chambers).
8. *Holtzman v. Schlesinger,* 414 U.S. 1316, 1317 (1973) (Douglas, J., in chambers).
9. Ibid.
10. Ibid.
11. *Holtzman v. Schlesinger,* 414 U.S. 1321 (1973) (Marshall, J., in chambers).
12. *Holtzman v. Schlesinger,* 414 U.S. 1321, 1324 (1973) (Douglas, J., in chambers).
13. "Judiciary and Judicial Procedure," Title 28 *U.S. Code,* Sec. 1, 2012.

Chapter 4: L'Affaire Agnew

1. Richard M. Nixon, *RN: The Memoirs of Richard Nixon* (New York: Grosset & Dunlap, 1978), 816.
2. Alexander M. Haig, Jr., and Charles McCarry, *Inner Circles: How America Changed the World* (New York: Warner, 1992), 351.
3. Ibid.
4. Ibid.
5. Nixon, *RN: The Memoirs of Richard Nixon,* 913.
6. Ibid.
7. Haig and McCarry, *Inner Circles,* 355.
8. Nixon, *RN: The Memoirs of Richard Nixon,* 914.
9. Ibid.
10. Aaron Latham, "Seven Days in October," *New York Magazine,* April 29, 1974, 41–58.

11. Fred Emery, *Watergate: The Corruption of American Politics and the Fall of Richard Nixon* (New York: Times, 1994), 301, 381.
12. Haig and McCarry, *Inner Circles*, 363.
13. Raoul Berger, *Impeachment: The Constitutional Problems* (Cambridge, Mass.: Harvard University Press, 1974).
14. Latham, "Seven Days in October," 41.

Chapter 5: The Saturday Night Massacre

1. Joe Klein, *The Natural: The Misunderstood Presidency of Bill Clinton* (New York: Broadway Books, Random House, 2003), 95.
2. *Northern Securities Co. v. U.S.* 193 U.S. 197 (1904) (Holmes, O., in chambers).
3. Haig and McCarry, *Inner Circles*, 367–368.
4. The development of the Stennis compromise is discussed in Latham, "Seven Days in October," 42–44.
5. James Doyle, to whom I am indebted, provides the most comprehensive account of the events leading up to and following the Massacre in James Doyle, *Not Above the Law: The Battles of Watergate Prosecutors Cox and Jaworski* (New York: William Morrow, 1977).
6. Ibid., 46.

Epilogue

1. Oliver Wendell Holmes, *The Occasional Speeches of Justice Oliver Wendell Holmes*, edited by Mark Howe (Cambridge, Mass.: Harvard University Press, 1962), 28–31.
2. John Roberts, Senate Hearing Testimony, September 15, 2005, http://www.asksam.com/ebooks/releases.asp?doc_handle=1396382&file=JGRHearing.ask&query=little%20guy&search=yes.
3. Barack Obama, "Why Obama Voted Against Roberts," *Wall Street Journal*, June 2, 2009, http://online.wsj.com/article/SB124390047073474499.html.

4. Barack Obama, in Jesse Lee, "The President's Remarks on Justice Souter," The White House Blog, May 1, 2009, http://www.whitehouse.gov/blog/09/05/01/The-Presidents-Remarks-on-Justice-Souter.
5. "The Bork Hearings; An Intellectual Appetite," *New York Times*, September 20, 1987, http://www.nytimes.com/1987/09/20/us/the-bork-hearings-an-intellectual-appetite.html.

INDEX

INDEX

INDEX